Praise for

'Ian's story is a g.... ...
he tells it really well' **Pete Paphides**

'All Ian Broudie's great gifts as a songwriter – melody,
vulnerability, empathy, hope – turn out to be in his
prose too. A lovely read' **David Baddiel**

'Brilliant . . . it's a beautiful book' **Dermot O'Leary**

'The best start to an autobiography I've read. I've got
"Pure" on a loop this morning' **Bonehead, Oasis**

'His excellent new memoir *Tomorrow's Here Today* reads like one
of his own songs: full of heart and sparkling melancholy. It contains highly entertaining, often self-deprecating stories about a
journey that began immersed in the thriving Liverpool punk
scene of the late '70s that was populated with an improbable
number of future pop stars' *i*

'He tells an enthralling tale with the wide-eyed wonder of an
innocent bystander. *Tomorrow's Here Today* is a pure delight'
Classic Pop ★★★★

'Not only is Broudie a terrific gossip, his ability to capture
what music has given him is heroic. Funny and revealing'
Record Collector ★★★★

'He may appear quiet, but it would be wrong to think
that he does not have strong opinions. What comes over
from this book is how driven he is when it comes to music.

Each chapter sounds as if Ian is talking directly to you. Revealing . . . [and] sharply observational'
Louder Than War

'[A] hilarious and touching memoir' ***Daily Express***

'One of the greatest rock 'n' roll stories of the past fifty years recounted with warmth and wisdom' ***Hot Press***

'A fascinating memoir . . . there are points in the book where you suddenly find yourself moving in deep water. Love, loss, grief. The stuff of being human' ***Sunday Post***

TOMORROW'S HERE TODAY

TOMORROW'S HERE TODAY

Lightning Seeds, Football and Cosmic Post-Punk

IAN BROUDIE

With John Higgs

NINE
EIGHT
BOOKS

NINE
EIGHT
BOOKS

NEB 022 PB

First published in the UK in 2023
This paperback edition published in 2024 by Nine Eight Books
An imprint of Black & White Publishing Group
A Bonnier Books UK company
4th Floor, Victoria House, Bloomsbury Square, London, WC1B 4DA
Owned by Bonnier Books, Sveavägen 56, Stockholm, Sweden

 @nineeightbooks

 @nineeightbooks

Paperback ISBN: 978-1-7887-0906-4
eBook ISBN: 978-1-7887-0904-0
Audio ISBN: 978-1-7887-0905-7

A CIP catalogue record for this book is available from the British Library.

Publishing director: Pete Selby
Editor: James Lilford

Top image on p. 4 of plate section © Mike Roberts
Image on p. 5 of plate section © Amanda Rose/Alamy
All other plate-section images courtesy of the author
Typeset by IDSUK (Data Connection) Ltd
Printed and bound in Great Britain by Clays Ltd, Elcograf S.p.A

1 3 5 7 9 10 8 6 4 2

Nine Eight Books is an imprint of Bonnier Books UK
www.bonnierbooks.co.uk

MIX
Paper | Supporting
responsible forestry
FSC® C018072

Ian Broudie originally emerged from the post-punk Liverpool music scene of the late '70s, playing in the band Big in Japan. Before the band ended, they created the indie label Zoo Records, which in turn led to Ian producing for an array of high-profile bands (sometimes credited with the pseudonym 'Kingbird').

Releasing his first record under the name 'Lightning Seeds' – the imaginary group he had envisioned when he wrote his songs in the hope it would become a reality – Ian went on to find considerable success as the band's frontman, culminating in the history-making 'Three Lions'.

Ian's studio is now located in Liverpool and he continues to write, record and produce material for the Lightning Seeds and as a soloist.

'Dreams, reality and recollection can sometimes be fickle partners in my head, but this is how I remember it . . .'

CONTENTS

1

'PERFECT'

I was driving along Riverside Drive in Liverpool with my mum, not long after it opened. This is the route which goes along the river from Aigburth to the docks. My mum, who was quite old then, was watching the river go by. It was raining and the river was grey and brown, as you'd expect.

My mum said to me, 'Look at the river, there's no blue in it at all.' I said, 'Mum, it's the Mersey. Why would it be blue?' My mum said, 'Well, when I was little, we used to go down to the river, me and my brothers and sisters, and we used to swim in there a bit further up. The river was much cleaner then, and it did used to be blue.'

This was a shock to me. It had never occurred to me that the Mersey used to be blue. I'd always taken for granted that the Mersey was a dirty brown river. It was always something of a joke. In Liverpool, a used condom is called a Mersey Goldfish, and things like that. I didn't miss it being blue, because I had never seen it looking like that. But of course, someone older than me like my mum who remembered what it used to be like would totally miss that. It seemed a real shame to me. Of course, you have to be aware of it in order to miss it. It was not just that something had been lost. The knowledge of what had been lost was also lost.

This thought and the emotions that it brought up in me led to the beginning of my song 'Perfect'. 'See the river's filled with rain, I wish it could be blue again'. That comes from my mum, but then the song becomes about my own memories and wondering if they will one day be lost. Will anyone know that they existed? Will anyone miss them? In particular, I thought about those lost days as a seventeen-year-old on the long walk home from Eric's. That club lingers long in my psyche.

At the end of the night when we were kicked out of the club, I'd have to walk all the way across town to Aigburth to get home. It would be a long walk but there would be lots of us, to begin with at least. Along the way people would disappear into the flats. Sometimes there would just be me and this girl Cathy left, who I had a bit of a crush on. She was quite something. She used to have her face painted like

2

a punk. I thought she looked amazing. But I was always very shy, so I never told her that I liked her. Although I was working up to it.

As you walk down Princes Avenue, you get to the top of Ullet Road and there's a big block of flats there, a really tall thing. They're still there. She used to live near the top of those flats. We'd walk across town together and then she'd turn off and go into the flats, while I carried on walking home by myself. I'd never known anyone who lived in a high-rise flat before, so it added to her mystique. She lived up there, between the sky and earth, and you could see the plants on the window sills up there, which was her garden of sorts. All these stray memories found a place in the song – 'In towers high with time to fill, gardens on your window sill, in between the pavement and the sky.'

I noticed that she hadn't been around for a while. Then, one day, I heard the unthinkable news that she had fallen from those flats to her death. This hit me hard. It was a real shock. I really didn't know Cathy that well. We used to walk home together, but there were loads of us. Yet the finality of those events was something I had never experienced before, and the memory of that shock has stayed with me.

On those long walks home everyone was running around, talking and laughing. Everyone was buzzing, or at least that's how I remember it now. I sing about people waving

3

to the taxis as they whizzed past, and they certainly never stopped for us, which was the reason we were having to walk all the way across town to get home. It was annoying having to walk home at the time, but looking back at those moments, they now feel like an adventure, and there was something golden about them. Gradually as you got out of town people would start peeling off until there would be fewer and fewer of you, and you'd end up sitting in someone's garden, talking until it got light.

Often, the things that stay with you are moments that no one else experienced. Those memories are yours alone. They only have meaning for you and no one else would understand them. It was all about how when you were young you were not yet fully formed. You had all of life ahead of you, with all its possibilities – you just need to figure it out somehow. Then you gradually lose touch with the people you shared those moments with, as they find their own specific life paths.

The need to preserve those precious times is quite universal, I think. That's what 'Perfect' seems to be about. A lot of my songs are about trying to preserve a moment, before it is lost for good. Maybe a lot are about losing a memory or losing an innocence. They're about being scared of things going away. If a moment can be captured in a song, then on some level it's been safely preserved. They pass so quickly, those moments. When they happen, they are everything, but then you blink and suddenly it's decades later and they've gone: 'Now tomorrow's here today and yesterday's today just fades away.'

Looking back, my life doesn't feel like it was a string of events along a linear timeline – this happened, then that happened, then this happened, and so on. When your life is laid out like that, it becomes a story and a narrative is projected onto it. It might become a rags-to-riches story, perhaps, or a tragedy, or even a quest. That's what our minds do – they like stories and they try to turn our lives into them. But doing that does distort things. It gives too much weight to some events or people and it misses out others who were really important to you but who don't fit the structure.

When I look at my life, I don't see it as a narrative, I see it in terms of moments – those moments in time that are burnt into your memory because of how vivid or emotional they were when you experienced them. I don't think this is just me, either. I think most people experience life in this way. This is probably why I write songs to capture moments and stop them from becoming lost. My songs are about how I felt at particular times. To get that across, you have to try to take that moment apart and unpack it in order to understand it. You hope that when someone hears it, they are able to empathise and share what was a uniquely personal

5

experience, and make it their own. It's not easy and some songs do it better than others, yet when you think back to your favourite songs, you instantly know how they make you feel. The moment that they describe has been trapped in time, and passed on. They've been saved, really.

This is why when you hear a song that chimes with you, it means the world to you.

2

'PURE'

One afternoon in 1988 I stood in front of the radio in my flat in Liverpool. I was a bag of nerves. Normally I listened to the radio through the hi-fi system in the living room, but on that day, it seemed important that I listened on the little radio in the kitchen. The day before, I had received word that 'Pure', my first single, was going to be played on *Steve Wright in the Afternoon*.

This was a really big deal. The record had been out for ages, but it hadn't done anything. It had been released by an indie label, who had pressed up a few hundred copies, which were available for sale in Rough Trade. There was nowhere else you could buy it. Every week, I would receive a phone call to tell me how it was doing. One week it would be at number 102 in the charts, then it would go down to number 110 and then it would go all the way up to number ninety-four – or something like that. This went on for weeks. I'd be told that some bloke in Stoke played it on local radio and the label would press up another fifty in response. It got played at the Hacienda in Manchester and in random clubs, so it never entirely vanished, but it never did much either. It just drifted around. In contrast, the Steve Wright show was a big deal, even by the standards of BBC Radio 1. It had 7.5 million listeners. If he was to play it, then the whole country would hear my song.

It felt like my big break. Although this was only my first record, it was probably also my last chance. You're supposed to release your first record when you're nineteen or so, when you are still full of bravado and energy. I was thirty-one. By the unwritten rules of the music business, I was already past it. I was also about to become a husband and a father and enter a new, more settled stage of life. The release of this single felt like the last throw of the dice.

So there I was the next afternoon, listening to the show. I sat through all the chart hits and traffic news, not really believing that it would happen. Then, suddenly, without an introduction, I heard those familiar opening notes. This time, they were coming from the radio, not from my tape player. That may have been a small detail, but it changed them completely. Steve Wright was playing my song! But halfway through, he stopped it. He took the needle off the record. He said something like, 'Hang on a minute, what is this?'

The moment the record began, it had all become real for me. I was so thrilled to hear 'Pure' coming out of my kitchen radio. At that point, it would never have occurred to me that he might change his mind and take it off. It was as if a joke had been played on me – I'd been set up to think that the best possible thing was going to happen and then the rug had been pulled out from under my feet. It was all a cruel trick and after being so pleased with myself, I was about to be humiliated in the most public way imaginable.

I stood there, staring at the radio, waiting to see what he said next and hear how he justified what he'd just done. I thought that he was going to declare that my record was not up to the standard of music which could be played on the BBC. The reason I thought that was because, deep down, I feared that it was true. Most records then were made by professional musicians in proper recording studios. I had recorded this song by myself and it had been largely done in my spare room. I also knew that what he was playing was unfinished.

What happened was this: I had spent most of the '80s working as a record producer, almost by accident. As the years went on, I'd become increasingly dissatisfied with the role. I'd worked with some unique and brilliant bands like the Fall, Shack and Echo & the Bunnymen and I'd been involved in some great records, but deep down I just didn't want to be a producer. I wanted to be a songwriter and a guitarist. I'd lost the feeling you get from making your own music, and it's only when you lose something like that that you realise how important it is.

When I was working with the Pale Fountains, I met this guy called Dick Leahy. He was an old-school '60s kind of music publisher guy – wealthy, big cigar, the sort of person you'd see in the background of photos of Keith Richards in his prime. Very likeable, very charming, he was your typical lovable rogue. He said to me, 'I really like these records you're producing and the sounds you're making. Surely this is writing. Have you got any of your own songs?' I said no and he said that if ever I had, I should give him a shout.

Some time passed and eventually I reached what felt like a breaking point. I thought of myself as a songwriter, but I wasn't writing any songs. My excuse was that I was trying to find the right band, yet it was looking increasingly unlikely that the right band was suddenly going to appear and knock on my door. But if I was producing and not writing any songs, then what right did I have telling myself that I was still a songwriter? It might sound daft, but my sense of identity was cracking. The only way out of this dilemma was to bite the bullet and write my own music.

It was quite a risk for me in a way. At the time there were loads of bands in Liverpool getting signed, like Rain, the Real People, the La's – all those great bands. The major labels were putting a lot of money behind the most promising local talent. But I didn't have a band. I didn't have a singer. I didn't have a manager. All I could do was some home recordings of my first songs. I didn't see myself as a frontman and I didn't think I had a frontman's voice, but I had to sing on those demos because there was no one else to do it.

I did versions of 'Pure' and a few other songs at home. I had the offer of some downtime at Amazon Studios in Kirkby because I had produced the Bunnymen album there. They told me I could go in and mix my tracks for free at night when there was no one else booked in. I went over with the tracks from home and did some presentable mixes of those first few songs. When I'd finished, they were the first songs that I'd ever completed on my own.

When I was in the studio, I sat down and wrote out the lyrics to 'Pure' and I realised that there were too many of them. There was something about the emotion that the song described which made all those words pour out of me. The mass of lyrics was the opposite of the song's key line,

11

which was 'Pure and simple every time'. I thought, 'There's way too many words for a song here. I've made a mistake, I've done it wrong.' I said to Cenzo the engineer, 'Forget that one, it's wrong. Just scrap it.'

With hindsight, I now think that part of the reason I took against 'Pure' was because it was the first song I'd written that was unmistakably personal. I was uncomfortable about that; I felt that I'd given something of myself away on that song. 'Pure' is a love song and I wasn't used to publicly saying that I was in love. It was about how I felt about my partner Becky and that was private. Often when singers in songs say 'I love you', it's done as a big powerful declarative thing. In real life, it can be a bit more awkward and embarrassing – something that you'd rather not say, but which you have to because it's a fact and you can't pretend otherwise. In 'Pure', I sing 'And I love you' in quite an underplayed way and I think some people identify with that and are moved by that. Afterwards, when I saw how they reacted to that song, I realised that making yourself vulnerable when you're writing a song is the whole point. It's the act of giving a part of yourself away that animates the song – that's what sparks it into life.

I asked Cenzo to ditch the song, but he said, 'No, I really like it. I'm going to put it down on the DAT anyway.' He put it at the start of this digital audio tape in its unfinished and abandoned form. All of the song's intro wasn't supposed to be there. The beginning, with the synths repeatedly going 'bah-ba, bah-ba' and the guitars noodling, that was just me getting ready and getting in time. If I'd finished the song properly, it would all have been cut off, which of course would have been a giant mistake. When 'Pure' was eventually played on the radio, that intro became the thing that made the song stand out. But I didn't understand that then – I still saw the whole beginning as just me mucking around.

Afterwards, I sent a cassette of these songs to Dick Leahy. I didn't really know what else to do with them. Sometime later, Dick called. He said to me, 'I'm sitting in my back garden, the sun is shining. I've got a bottle of Chablis and I'm enjoying a cold glass of wine. I'm playing your song. I've listened to it a few times and I love it. You know, I really love this song. Let's put it out.' I said, 'Okay, how should we go about this? Should we get a record deal?' He said, 'Oh, let's not be too hasty. I'll just have 500 pressed up and I'll hire someone to take it into the radio stations. We'll sell it at Rough Trade and we'll see how it goes.' I thought, 'Well, this isn't going to make my life any different.' I think he had about 200 pressed up in the end.

The whole thing was very casual and shambolic. From my first batch of songs, there were two that I thought were the strongest, which might make good singles. Those were 'Pure' and 'All I Want'. After Dick said that he was going to test release 'Pure' as a single, I thought that 'All I Want' should be the second single. After I was sent a copy of 'Pure', however, I saw that he'd put 'All I Want' on the B-side. That was my strongest other song and it had just been thrown away. There hadn't been any conversations about this or any proper strategy. There hadn't been any money or time to even finish the song properly – it was just 'throw it out there and see if anything happens'. There was no real promotion, other than a record plugger called Scott that Dick had hired.

When I got the call saying that my song was going to be played, it seemed too good to be true. Then Steve Wright stopped the record halfway through and he took it off. I was stuck in that moment where your dream is about to burst and there's absolutely nothing you can do about it. Steve said, 'Who is this – the Lightning Seeds? I've never heard of them. Who are the Lightning Seeds?' Which was fair enough. But then he said, 'This is fantastic. I'm gonna play it from the beginning again!' Which no one ever did. He put it on from the beginning and at the end, he said, 'Isn't that wonderful? I'm going to play it again.' And he did. Again, this was not usual. People started phoning up the BBC, asking about it. It was unbelievable. And at that moment my future clicked into place.

After this, lots of other stations noticed the song and put it on their playlists. It promptly sold out, so Dick had to get some more records pressed up. Then it crept up the charts enough for me to be offered *Top of the Pops*. Of course, I didn't have a band or anything, but I'd done a video that was just me on my own sat on a stool by some bushes. They showed that instead and after the video had been on *Top of the Pops*, Rough Trade promptly ran out of records again. It never became a massive hit because people couldn't easily get a copy. But they had heard the song and they wanted it, and that in itself was thrilling for me.

Shortly after this I was alone in my flat in Liverpool when the phone rang. I answered it and this big American voice boomed, 'Is this Ian from the Lightning Seeds? This is Rodney Bingenheimer in LA on K-ROQ – Rodney on the ROQ! You're the most-requested record in California!' And I was like, 'Who is this? Who's messing about?' The voice goes, 'It's me, it's Rod!' I said, 'Well, it can't be, mate, because I haven't got a record deal in America. It's not out there.' He said, 'Exactly! That's why it's the most-requested record on the West Coast!'

It turned out Rodney Bingenheimer had been over in London at Portobello Market and he heard the record and bought a copy from Rough Trade. He took it back to California and started playing it on his show. Soon, other radio stations imported it and were playing it too. Apparently, it was all over the radio in California.

Thinking about all that now, it doesn't really seem plausible, does it? What would be the chances that a big LA DJ would be wandering down Portobello Market and pick up on your song like that? But that's 'Pure' for you. After Rodney started pushing it, the song was released properly over there by MCA. That was a deal that Dick Leahy set up, which I didn't have a say in, but thankfully MCA kept 'All I Want' off the B-side so that it could be used as the follow-up single. 'Pure' really took off through radio plays alone and it made the *Billboard* chart. To this day, it's still my biggest American hit.

I've often said that I much prefer songs before they're finished. You lose something when you complete a song. Before you finish a record, it has all these possibilities, but as soon as it's defined, then it is what it is. It's no longer able to be anything else. The paradox here is that, in the end, you have to finish a song. It has to be completed to the stage where other people can hear it and it has to be sent out into the world, or else what's the point? It's your job to nail it down and define exactly what it is, even though that makes it limited and fixed, and closes off all those other avenues of potential. I think sometimes that because 'Pure' was never really finished, it managed to hold something special within it. Something pure, funnily enough. Perhaps that's why it chimes with people – they recognise that it's exactly what it claims to be.

Finishing a song is always a mixed feeling. It can leave you with something that you think is good, but in the back of your mind you're still aware of all the other directions that the song might have gone in, but didn't. Of course, unheard songs remain immune to criticism, and undefined, unfulfilled and unfinished things have a strange, alluring power. Potential is such an exciting thing. It draws you on and keeps you working, even though that potential is not part of the final work that you complete and manifest. I suppose this is a good thing because that disappointment is what makes you start writing the next song.

Years later, in 2009, I was a guest on the *Radcliffe & Maconie* show on BBC Radio 2 and there was a strange little echo of Steve Wright stopping 'Pure' halfway through. Mark Radcliffe was away for some reason. There was only Stuart Maconie presenting, so he had to do all the technical bits that DJs do himself. This meant that he'd ask me a question and he'd look at me while he asked it, but as soon as I started answering, he'd turn away and start doing other things. It felt like he wasn't interested and wasn't even pretending to be interested. I know that this is fairly normal in radio interviews and that I should have been together enough not to be fazed by it, but at the time it really put me off.

After chatting for a few minutes, I was set to perform an acoustic version of 'Pure'. It's quite a delicate song when it's done that way, just an acoustic guitar and my voice. I got about halfway through − probably close to the bit where Steve Wright had taken the record off − and I forgot the words. As I said, it's a song that has too many words. I had to stop: 'Do you know what? I've forgotten how it goes.' All this was live on radio.

There was a big panic in the studio. Stuart had to cover by doing another section of the show early. I left the booth and the producer was furious with me. She told me I was terrible, unprofessional, and I felt bad because I couldn't really argue with what she was saying. I mean, I'm supposed to be a singer. I should be able to sing a song all the way through. That's the minimum requirement of the job. I thought I'd better collect my guitar, sort out my things and slink off home.

By the time I'd got my stuff together, however, there had been a real change of mood in the producer's booth. Following my appearance, they had received a load of emails and phone calls from listeners who had been engrossed in the song and moved by both it and my failure. From the gist of the messages, it seemed that there had been something about my performance that people had related to: they found it really human. The producer, as a result, changed her tune. She stopped having a go at me and asked me to go back on the show. She wanted me to make another attempt at the song. So that's what I did: I went back on the show and made another pass at the song, and this time I made it all the way through. No one was looking disinterested this time.

The journalist Miranda Sawyer was listening to all this at home. She wrote about it in her radio review column in the *Observer* that week. She said that me coming back after forty-five minutes and managing to sing the song all the way through made her cry. 'It was so lovely,' she wrote, 'And I thought, how nice it was to hear some kindness on a radio show, a bit of space to let someone breathe out, recover their aplomb and do what they and we know they can.' If she'd have heard the bollocking I got from the producer, she might not have been so struck by the kindness, but her reaction, and the reaction of all the other listeners that wrote in, made the whole thing worthwhile. There is something about that song that wants to remain unfinished, or at least open to change. It doesn't seem to have become fixed, nailed down and exhausted. There's a mystery to it that I don't really understand.

I'm often surprised by how often music, and quite often my songs, makes people cry, especially when I'm not trying to. There have been many times when I've been writing a song and I play it to people and they unexpectedly become emotional. When I started writing the last album, *See You in the Stars* (2022), I met with my good friend Eric Longley and I played him the song 'Great to Be Alive'. That's the one that starts with the words, 'Hope lives in young men's hearts / It's the key to their charm / It keeps them from harm.' I felt that this was a really uplifting line, but he became tearful. I told him that the song wasn't supposed to have that effect. It's called 'Great to Be Alive', for heaven's sake. But it had hit a chord emotionally. Those opening lines have an impact on people because in this culture you don't really get young men being spoken about in those terms. It would be lovely if you could properly manage what emotions a song is going to trigger, but no one can really control that. Doubtless, if you were really trying to write a song that would make people cry, chances are they will sit through the thing stony-faced.

I owe everything to 'Pure'. I'll always be grateful for it. That song has been a weird life-changing miracle for me. You couldn't have had a more serendipitous chain of events than those that led it to make its way out into the world. It was a miracle that I wrote it in the first place. I had no infrastructure whatsoever – no band, no promotion, no proper record deal. I tried to throw it away, but that didn't stop it.

I didn't finish it. I never properly mixed it. I didn't even top-and-tail it. But none of that mattered because the song itself was on a mission. The whole thing was just mad. It changed my life for ever.

It was the first song I ever wrote by myself. It's still the best thing I've ever done.

3

'BUT THEY'RE DEAD NICE'

As well as getting 'Pure' released in America by MCA, Dick Leahy also signed a deal with a small German label, and the record was released over there as well. Again, I only found out about this after the fact. It was all very disorganised. At this stage the Lightning Seeds were just me and a bunch of chancers who were winging it, basically. This German deal, however, did lead to my first overseas promotional trip. I got a message saying I had to get a flight to Bremen in north Germany. There, I'd be met by someone called Oliver, who would take me to a television studio. I would then mime to 'Pure' on German TV. The only problem was, they wanted me to bring a full band with me.

As we were only going to mime, this didn't need to be a real band. I was able to round up a bunch of mates who fancied a free trip to Germany and we formed a pretend version of the Lightning Seeds. My partner Becky agreed to be the keyboard player. She didn't actually play keyboards, but she was more than up to the task of pretending that she could. My mate Lloyd also agreed to come along as a pretend bass player. He proved to be such a natural at miming to my songs that I went on to put him in the videos we made for early Lightning Seeds singles. Then I phoned the drummer Chris Sharrock, who I met when I produced the Icicle Works, and asked him to help out. This proved to be prophetic, as Chris did actually join the Lightning Seeds for real a few years later when we finally became a touring band. Since then, he's gone on to play with the likes of Oasis, the La's and Robbie Williams.

So I had my pretend band and we flew off to Bremen. We got off the plane and found this Oliver waiting for us. Oliver was great. He looked like a dashing airline pilot from the '50s. We piled into his car and he took us to a hotel before heading to the television station for our big appearance. As we were standing under the hot lights in the TV studio, it occurred to me that we should have maybe practised miming to the song beforehand so that at least we would look convincing – I often have good ideas like this when it's much too late to do anything about them.

On our last night there, we were in a hotel in Hamburg. Me and Becky stayed in and turned in early, but Chris and Lloyd headed off to the Reeperbahn to make a night of it. Given the early history of the Beatles, Liverpool bands love to visit the Hamburg Reeperbahn. At some point in the evening, the phone went. I answered and it was Lloyd, and he sounded in a bit of a state.

'Lloyd, are you okay?' I asked.

'No. Chris has been kidnapped.'

'What? What do you mean?'

'I mean, Chris has been kidnapped!'

He explained that they had been wandering around the Reeperbahn and they'd gone into a club. They had a couple of drinks and some girls were talking to them, and they were having a lovely time. The girls would occasionally ask if they could have a drink and they would say, 'Sure!' Then they went to go and this huge bouncer stopped them. He said that they'd been buying the hostesses expensive drinks and that they had a huge bill to settle, the equivalent of hundreds of pounds. They didn't have anything like that on them so they said to the bouncer, 'We don't have that kind of money.' Then this bouncer got out a really big knife. He pointed it at Chris and said to Lloyd, 'This guy can't leave. You can leave. Go get the money and bring it here. If you do that, we'll let your friend go.'

That's when Lloyd rang me. He was really worried. He kept saying, 'I think they're going to stab Chris, I think they're going to kill him. What should we do?' I didn't know what to do. I didn't have that sort of money, or any way to get it. People didn't have debit or credit cards back then and I didn't know anyone in Germany who could have helped. Pretty much the only thing we could do was to go to the police. So I got dressed and left Becky in the room and went over to the Reeperbahn to find Lloyd.

There was a police station on one corner of the Reeperbahn, so we braced ourselves and went in. It was about eleven or twelve at night and it was absolute madness in there. All fights, prostitution and drunken screaming, it was a heavy, frightening place. The German police were all dressed in leather and armed with these really big guns. We were sitting there for ages waiting, but finally this English-speaking officer came to talk to us. We explained what had happened as best we could. It probably helped that I told him we were a band from Liverpool here to perform on television, as the people around the Reeperbahn are still very proud of their role in forging the Beatles. He said, 'Okay – wait here. We will get your friend back.'

After half an hour, a team of about half a dozen heavily armoured officers arrived. They were all huge – they looked more like the military than the police. We were told to get in the van with all these heavies. It drove off and Lloyd pointed out the nightclub. The squad left the van and I was told to go with them. They marched towards the entrance. The bouncers at the door went to stop them, but the police were ready for a ruck and they started pounding on these bouncers with their batons. So now we could all get into the club – Lloyd, myself and this fearsome army. I looked around and spotted Chris at a table near the back. He looked up, all surprised to see me.

'Hi, Ian!' he said. 'What are you doing here?'

I said, 'What do you mean, what am I doing here? We've come to rescue you.'

Chris looked surprised. He gestured at the guys he was talking to and he said, 'But they're dead nice!'

I had turned up with this paramilitary attack squadron, who were beating the crap out of the guys from the club, and Chris was just sitting there having a really nice time.

We were taken upstairs to see the main guy from the club, the one who had kidnapped Chris with the knife. The poor guy was sitting there surrounded by these police officers. He'd been hit on the head and was bleeding and dishevelled. This dazed German guy looked up at me – one of the least heavy-looking guys you could imagine. He said, in this little plaintive voice with these big, questioning eyes, 'Who *are* you?'

Because Chris was free to go and seemed perfectly happy, the police thought that we'd wasted their time. They'd knocked around all these club guys for no reason. As we were going back to the hotel, the chief officer asked me when we were leaving. I explained that we were flying back to the UK in the morning. He nodded, looked me in the eye and said in his gravelly German voice, 'You will not be welcome back.'

And that was my first experience of international promotion.

4

SENSE

In the wake of the attention that 'Pure' generated, I finished off a batch of songs which became my first album, *Cloudcuckooland* (1990). Dick Leahy's indie label, Ghetto Records, released this in the UK through Rough Trade, while MCA put it out in America. That record was me finding my feet, basically. I don't love that album in its entirety, but at the same time there are some songs and lots of moments that I am very proud of.

As an artist and as a singer, you have to find your voice. This album was that for me. I was seeing what I could do. I was trying to move away from a generic band sound and become something uniquely me. And I did find it, in moments. A song like 'Bound in a Nutshell' – as much as I love that lyric –

wouldn't have fitted on any of my later albums and neither would 'The Nearly Man', which is another song I really like. They're good songs, but they're not quite what I wanted the Lightning Seeds to be. 'All I Want' and 'Pure', in contrast, were exactly it, and they would have fitted on any of the albums that were to come. In those two songs I felt I had succeeded in defining what the Lightning Seeds were. It was not grim northern raincoat indie. There was a lot of that around at the time. It was intended to be psychedelic, uplifting pop. I loved early Pink Floyd and songs like 'See Emily Play', and I thought that I'd love to get close to that sort of sound.

With *Cloudcuckooland* and the single 'Pure', I felt that I had made a promising start, but I still needed to build on that momentum and not let it fizzle out. Very quickly I got to work on the songs that would make up *Sense* (1992), my second album. I still hoped that the Lightning Seeds would become a cooperative, and that collaborators would appear and help me work on different songs. But those mythical collaborators never really arrived.

What I was really hoping for was a singer. I sung the vocals on the first album out of necessity, even though I found it pretty difficult. That was no reason why the second album couldn't be different. A really good singer, I knew, would be the most effective way of lifting the Lightning Seeds' recordings up a level. I was looking for a female vocalist in particular. I auditioned a few, but the right person proved elusive. During this time I was also writing the songs, and the better ones seemed so personal that, reluctantly, I started to accept that I was the one who should be singing them. 'The Life of Riley' is a good example. I started writing it when Becky was pregnant and finished it after our son Riley was born. With such a personal lyric as that, it just seemed wrong to get someone else to sing it.

Although I was much more of a one-man band than I wanted to be in the studio, I could at least collaborate with different songwriters. I'd done this from the very start, which was quite rare in those days. I can't remember anyone else in Liverpool writing with people who weren't in their band. On the first album, I wrote a track with Peter Coyle from the Lotus Eaters and one with Richard Jobson from Skids. For the second album, I wrote 'Happy' with Ian McNabb and three songs with Terry Hall, including the title song. Writing songs with Terry would prove to be a pleasure and a privilege, and one of the great strengths of the Lightning Seeds going forwards.

At the time, the major labels had taken a great interest in Liverpool bands. They would come up and see gigs all the time, but unfortunately, as there was just me, there were no Lightning Seeds gigs for them to see. I'd largely recorded the first album in my flat, along with snatched moments in studios. For the second album, I stayed with the idea of home recording, which I found comfortable and creative. My oldest brother Robert had just split up with his girlfriend, and when she left, she took pretty much all of the furniture with her. This meant that there was an entirely empty room in his house. I asked him if I could use it for a week to record my next album in. He agreed and, needless to say, I was in there for months.

Looking back at this now, I realise how nice it was of him to allow me to do that. At the time, I was so focused on my new songs that I never consciously acknowledged what he was doing for me. His house was a bit of an odd shape and this empty room made an ideal studio, so it seemed perfectly reasonable to me to hole up in there making all that noise for weeks on end. There was a ten-year age gap between me and Robert and it could be difficult for us to connect. Now I'm older, and hopefully wiser, I realise that the problem was me just as much as it was him, and now I recognise how kind he was to let me use his house like that. I feel sad now because I don't think I appreciated what he did for me. It just used to annoy me that he kept coming in when I was trying to work, and I wish I'd thanked him properly.

Musically, the way I worked changed around *Sense*. There were two main reasons for this. The first was because samplers had been invented and the second was because

I'd heard De La Soul. I studied the way they used loops to build up their tracks and I thought it sounded amazing, especially compared to the cheap drum machine I had used on *Cloudcuckooland*. I started to wonder if I could do something similar and construct songs, rather than just a groove, using that way of working. The idea was exciting because I didn't know if it was possible or not. By that time, though, I'd met Simon Rogers, who used to play bass in the Fall: he had a sampler and, even rarer, he knew how to use it.

What Simon and I did was basically sample things off records, particularly drums. There are no real drums on that album. It's all sampled beats from all sorts of old records, from Stevie Wonder to Otis Redding, and everything in between. At that time, this was pretty much a hip-hop only way of working, and there was a fair bit of luck and trial and error involved in making it all fit in the right key. The technology to do this wasn't there like it is now. It was difficult, but it was engrossing.

The way the album was recorded was driven by both necessity and curiosity, which is quite a potent combination. There is something unbelievably satisfying about getting a song to work in those situations. The end result worked particularly well on the track 'Sense', which at the time sounded quite striking.

Thanks to 'Pure' and 'All I Want', I was fortunate enough to go into that album already knowing what it should sound like. I got there at times, but not with every song. The singles 'The Life of Riley' and 'Sense' were bullseyes, as far as I was concerned, and I think I got closer to what I was aiming for on the second album than I did on the first. But, ultimately, I wasn't quite there yet: I could see where I wanted to go, but I was still wrestling with the skills needed to achieve it.

For the first album, Dick Leahy had reached a deal to release it through Rough Trade records. They went bust shortly afterwards, so if that record had made any money we never saw it. For the second album, he did a deal where he basically sold me to Virgin. Again, I didn't really have a say in this, but it looked like it could work out okay and that I might even get some money. The week before the single 'Sense' was due to come out, however, Richard Branson sold Virgin Records to Thorn EMI. Loads of people at Virgin lost their jobs, including the ones who were the champions of my music inside that company.

On the plus side, however, I'd found a new way of working. I had proved to myself that I could achieve what I wanted to achieve with that process. From the start, I had always seen the Lightning Seeds as a three-album project. With the next album, maybe I would finally get it right.

5

'HE WON'T BE JOINING YOU'

After the interest in 'Pure' from American radio, Dick Leahy introduced me to Susan Dodes, a really lovely A&R executive from New York. She came up to Liverpool and we got on immediately. I could tell she genuinely loved that song and completely understood what it was that I was trying to do. After she signed me to MCA, I was invited to meet her boss, who was about to fly back to London from America. This was an English guy called Paul Atkinson. I was excited by this because Paul used to be the guitarist in the Zombies.

I loved the Zombies and especially their 1968 album, *Odessey and Oracle*, so I was thrilled to have a chance to meet him. I knew I would have to check myself at the meeting and hold back from just quizzing him at length about *his band* instead of talking about what I was doing. I had no idea that he'd become an A&R man, moved to America or was working at MCA. These were the days before the internet, so you couldn't keep track of what people were up to in the same way that you can now. The plan was that me and Dick Leahy would meet Paul for dinner, so I got the train down from Liverpool in order to meet him in London.

Dick and I arrived at the Italian restaurant in Soho on time, and we sat down and waited for Paul to arrive. We waited, and waited, but he didn't turn up. It was starting to get a bit odd and awkward. We couldn't work out if something had happened to him, if we'd been stood up or, being an American A&R man, if Paul was being deliberately late as some weird power move. Then the waiter came over and asked if we were ready to order. We told him we were still waiting for somebody. The waiter asked if the person was Mr Atkinson. We said that it was and he said, 'Mr Atkinson is having dinner with some people over there. He just wanted to buy you dinner, but he won't be joining you.'

Me and Dick just looked at each other. I think we were both checking that we both found this equally insane. We'd never heard of anything like this before and we were trying to get our heads around it. Was this something that happened, which other people were fine with, or was it just unbelievably rude? We looked over and there he was, dining with a group of people who were presumably more interesting or important than we were. Then he came over and basically repeated what the waiter had told us: he'd come over from America and wanted to buy us dinner, but he was with some other people and he couldn't join us. Then he went off.

That was my first encounter with American label bosses and the experience has never been topped. I thought, 'I've just come all the way down here on the train. Does he think I can't buy my own bowl of pasta?' We just got up and left.

Paul not meeting us or getting to know who I was would have consequences later. Susan Dodes managed to sign us to MCA and 'Pure' made it onto the *Billboard* chart. They released *Cloudcuckooland* and were preparing to release *Sense*. This led to a transatlantic conference call with Paul and all the MCA team. They were all sat around a speaker at a conference table in an office in LA in the morning, while I was on the phone in my flat in Liverpool at night. As you can imagine, there was a lot of that American corporate gushing to wade through, about how much they loved you and what a genius you were. I know I shouldn't really complain about things like that, but it does feel very weird when you come from a place like Liverpool.

They then started to go through their plans to promote me and the album. They were excited about the potential they saw for the Lightning Seeds in America. The next step would be to get me over and to tour there soon. They were 'super-excited', they explained, to help organise a tour for me. The question was, when would me and my band be able to come over? I told them that I didn't have a band, it was just me. They said okay, this wasn't a problem. They could put a group together around me and I could tour America that way. At this point, I said, 'I'm not sure I could do that. I wouldn't be very comfortable – I've never sung in front of people before.'

There then followed the longest silence of any telephone call I've ever known.

Maybe now this wouldn't seem that strange. There's a 21st-century tradition of producers making music in their bedrooms and there are ways to market them. At the time, however, if you weren't a band and you didn't tour, then they had no idea what to do with you. I just didn't fit into the way the music industry was then set up. The industry worked on the assumption that bands get together, rehearse, gig, go into the studio and then have hits. I would ultimately do all these things, but in reverse order. I do seem unable to do things in the correct way. With hindsight, it probably would have been a really good move to go over and tour America properly on the back of a hit, while I still had all that radio support. It probably would have set my life up in a very different way to how things turned out.

Susan Dodes was a very astute A&R person. Although based in America, she had clocked that there was a lot of interesting stuff coming out of the north of England and that I was pretty well connected to it. She asked me if I would be interested in having my own label. The idea was that I would find a bunch of local bands who I could then record and they would set up the label for me as an imprint of MCA. I thought this sounded great, so I immediately put the word out that I was looking for bands.

My friend Phil Saxe, who had been an A&R man at Factory, played me a demo of Pulp. I really liked what I heard. Then there was a Manchester band that I really liked called the Sugar Merchants. They later changed their name to Audioweb and had a hit with a cover of 'Bankrobber' by the Clash. The third band I wanted was suggested to me by keyboardist Clint Boon of the Inspiral Carpets. He sent me a tape of some mates of his: they were called Oasis.

I sent the tapes off to Paul Atkinson in America and I waited. He was going to listen to what I'd come up with and, if he thought that there was any potential in an MCA label with Pulp, the Sugar Merchants and Oasis, then he would give the project the go-ahead.

On the face of it, the years I was with MCA in America were good for me. They are still the high point of my career in the US. They released my first two albums and all the singles from those records – 'Pure', 'All I Want', 'Sense' and 'The Life of Riley' – were big radio hits. I doubt things like the song 'Change' being used in the film *Clueless* (1995) would have happened without those records preparing the ground for me over there. But ultimately, I wasn't right in MCA's eyes. I didn't make sense to them; I wasn't what a band should be. Susan Dodes was genuinely supportive, but I don't think Paul Atkinson would have agreed to sign me if he had sat down with us in that Soho restaurant and got to know who I was and what I did.

On Christmas Eve 1992, I was in my flat on Beaconsfield Road with Becky. We were getting ready for the following day, which becomes more of a big event when you have a young child. Riley was still too little to know what Christmas was, but to parents that doesn't matter. You tend to go overboard regardless. Christmas becomes a more magical time, even before the little one understands it. Then the phone rang. A voice said that Paul Atkinson was phoning from LA and asked me to hold the line. I waited and after a weirdly long time he came on the phone. He said, 'Hello, Ian. We've been talking about what to do with you and because you don't play live, we don't know how to move you on to the next level. So I'm just giving you a ring to say we're dropping you. And thanks for sending over those demo tapes, but we won't be moving forward with the label idea.' Then he rang off.

I said to Becky, 'They've just dropped me with a phone call . . . on Christmas Eve!'

On some level, I was still pretty much in the same place as where I started. I had no band, no management, no infra-structure and no record label. No one was phoning or ask-ing me to do things. I had no upcoming commitments. The Lightning Seeds only existed if I said they did and if I forgot all about them no one would have complained. At the same time, I had a young family to support and I could only do that by taking on more producing jobs. With Paul's Christmas Eve call, the first stage of the Lightning Seeds' story came to an end. He had also turned down a chance to sign Oasis and I never did get to tell him how much I loved *Odessey and Oracle*.

Fortunately, my Zombies fandom had a nice ending. About five years later, I had a studio of my own in part of a large building in a rundown part of Liverpool. I was in there on a freezing cold winter's day and I left my studio to head to the shops. As I went out of the building, I noticed this guy standing around in the hallway. He was still there when I came back, so I said, 'Are you alright, mate?' He told me he was waiting for some people in an upstairs studio. I said, 'Do you want to come in for a cup of tea while you're waiting? Because you look fucking freezing.'

I made him a cup of tea and he got warmed up. He told me that he was there to do an interview. At that time there was a radio station called Crash FM, which was quite a hip thing. Janice Long used to DJ on it and it was sort of a precursor to XFM. They sometimes used a part of the building to record interviews. Then he told me his name was Colin and the penny finally dropped: this was Colin Blunstone, lead singer of the Zombies. I told him I was a massive fan. I just couldn't believe it – Colin Blunstone was sitting on my couch. We had a good old chat and he was lovely. Then someone arrived and he went off and did his interview.

It's a very special memory for me – I'm glad I got to tell a Zombie how much I loved their work.

6

'THE BACK OF LOVE'

A decade before all this, on a winter's day in January 1980, I was waiting at a bus stop on Smithdown Road in the rain, trying to get home, when a blue transit pulled up. Inside the van were Echo & the Bunnymen, and they offered me a lift to Penny Lane.

I say it was Echo & the Bunnymen, but in truth I think it was just three of them. There was Les Pattinson, their bassist, who was driving. Next to him sat guitarist Will Sergeant and their singer, Ian McCulloch. We all called him 'McCull' at the time, but now he's just 'Mac'. These were the original three members of the band. Their drum machine Echo had recently been replaced by the wonderful Pete de Freitas, but for whatever reason he wasn't in the van with them that day.

Pete was a lovely guy, and an unbelievable drummer. It spoiled me really because the first two drummers I got to know and work with were Pete de Freitas and Budgie, and they were world-beaters. It made it hard for me to work with some other drummers after that. Pete completed the Bunnymen. Before they found him they had played for a while with a very temperamental drum machine. That was okay, but when Pete arrived, he transformed the band into this perfect thing.

Pete was from Somerset, not Liverpool, so we thought he was quite posh and maybe a little naive. They were all quite innocent, the Bunnymen – they weren't hipsters or cynics, despite how cool they looked. I remember being at one of their first rehearsals with Pete. We had a break and he ventured out for a wander around Liverpool. When he came back, he was very excited and carrying a beaten-up old Ludwig drum. He said, 'I've had a real stroke of luck! I met this guy who had Ringo's old drum and he let me buy it off him!' We were sceptical to say the least.

The van had windows down the side like a small bus, but there were no seats in the back. Sometimes they would put deckchairs in there and they would travel very comfortably that way, but I squeezed into the front seats with the rest of them. The Bunnymen had just signed to the Korova label and were in the process of becoming a more committed and professional outfit. To prove it, Les had just bought himself some transport.

We drove off and I noticed that they had a tape playing. 'What's this?' I asked, and they said, 'It's us. We've just recorded a load of stuff in a proper studio, but we're not sure if we like it.' They were driving around, listening to it. During the drive down to Penny Lane I heard a couple of songs. I was a friend and a fan. I'd seen them play their early gigs, and, knowing how great they were live, I was a little disappointed by the recordings.

I probably overstepped the mark by telling them my unsolicited thoughts. I said that a couple of arrangements could be better, some of the best bits only happened once, and some of the best guitar lines seemed buried. I instantly bit my tongue and wished that I hadn't said anything, got out the van, and thanked them for the lift.

Unbeknown to me, that little conversation would eventually change the course of my life. A few days later, I got a call from their manager Bill Drummond out of the blue. Bill was an older Scottish guy, and he and I had been in a band together called Big in Japan, so we knew each other pretty well. Later on, of course, Bill would go on to notoriety as half of the KLF, and he also burnt a million quid on a Scottish island for no good reason, which is probably what he's best remembered for. Bill said, 'The Bunnymen were saying you had a few ideas about the songs they played you – would you fancy producing a couple of tracks?' I said, 'Yeah, I'd love to go in a studio with them. I've never produced anything before, but how hard can it be?' Thinking back, it seemed quite a casual thing. A couple of weeks later, we were in Eden Studios in London recording the songs 'Rescue' and 'Pride'.

I was just all in. They were my friends, and I was a little in awe of them. It was as if I joined the band for a period to help out. There weren't any great divisions of roles between us. I'd play a bit of guitar or help with the arrangements and the parts, or just do whatever needed doing. We were all on the same page, working on this record together. It just happened that for some reason I was the one who best understood the technical stuff, like where to put the microphones or how to get the best sound, things like that. The funny thing is, I don't know now how I knew all that back then. It was all very instinctive. I just went into the studio for the first time and I did it, and it felt like I had always been able to do it. It just happened in the moment.

I think the record turned out really well, and I was very happy. It sounded like the Bunnymen and no one else: we'd captured a little bit of what was magic about them. For my first attempt at producing, it was a good experience and a win.

For the next year or two, I was living in London playing in a band called Original Mirrors. I wasn't giving any thought to any more production, as I was off on tour around Europe supporting Roxy Music.

When that chapter came to a close and I resurfaced in Liverpool, I shared a flat with Will Sergeant for a couple of years. Will was then, and is now, one of my favourite people to be around. He's quite eccentric and can be an awkward character, but he has a beautiful stubbornness that serves him well musically and makes everything he does unique. There's a great quote, 'There's no such thing as a wrong note if you mean it,' and that sums up Will perfectly.

The Bunnymen were now about to record their third album, which would become *Porcupine* (1983), and I received a call from Bill Drummond asking me if I'd be up for producing it. I was bit conflicted by the idea. I saw myself as a songwriter, and producing the now-established Echo & the Bunnymen sounded like a serious responsibility and a shift in focus that I wasn't anticipating. My first reaction was to say, 'Probably not.' To me, it felt like it would be crossing a line. I saw it as a poacher-turned-gamekeeper situation. When you're a producer, you're working for the record company. I really felt that my loyalties lay with the artist.

But Bill being Bill, he phoned me back a few days later with a strangely surreal idea. He said, 'What about if you didn't produce it, but you had an alter ego and your alter ego produced it? Do you have an alter ego?' I replied, 'Funny you should mention it. I was recently christened Kingbird by a friend of mine called Chris.'

Chris was a little bit older than me. He was on a lot of medication, which he tended to use creating huge wild paintings. He had called round to my mum's house looking for me, in quite an agitated state. When my mum told him I was out, he asked her to pass on this message, which she duly did. She told me that Chris called round and asked her to tell me that he was worried that there was going to be a nuclear explosion pretty soon, and that he had access to two asbestos suits, and I was to give him a call urgently regarding the asbestos suits. 'Oh, and by the way,' she said, 'he told me to tell you that you are Kingbird.' I said, 'I don't know what that means, Mum.'

When I saw Chris next, he had forgotten all about this. I never got an explanation as to what it meant, but there was something about the name that appealed and I did wonder what it would mean to be Kingbird.

Bill said, 'Great, that's settled, then. Let's get Kingbird to produce the album.' That's why, if you look at those early Bunnymen records I did with them, they say this was a Kingbird production rather than including my name.

The first song we recorded was 'The Back of Love'. The band had played this song, under the original title 'Taking Advantage', on a John Peel session, and Korova were quite excited about it.

In rehearsals, I made some changes. We sped the song up significantly, which toughened the whole sound and made it extremely exciting. This was hard on poor Pete because he had come up with an amazing, but quite complicated, drum beat for the song, which he played with his arms crossed. He was such a great drummer though that he could still make it work even after I had sped the song right up, which was no mean feat. Mac and I had been listening to a lot of Jacques Brel, and we decided that it would be a great idea if he sang it in a style somewhere between Jacques Brel and Johnny Rotten, spitting out the lyric and rolling his 'r's in quite a manic way. This instantly seemed to fit.

I added some very aggressive swooping cellos, and a *Psycho*-like string motif for the middle eight. It was the first time that I'd worked with session string parts and I had to whistle and hum all the parts because I can't write them out musically, which they weren't entirely happy about. Years later, Mac was asked in an interview about whose idea it was to put cellos on 'The Back of Love'. There had never been any strings on Bunnymen records before and it had come to be seen as a defining moment in crafting the classic

Bunnymen sound. He replied, 'Oh, that was my idea.' When I saw him next, I was quick to challenge him on this: 'My recollection was that it was my idea to use cellos and I scored them and recorded them, and mixed them. How was it your idea?' With a surprised look on his face, he said, 'But I told you it needed something.' And to give him his due, he did say that: he did tell me that it needed something.

Will, Les and Pete were really uneasy about the lyric that Mac had written for the chorus, which included the word 'love'. They was an unwritten understanding that singing about love was exactly the sort of thing the Bunnymen should avoid. But Mac insisted. 'It's not love,' he said. 'This is the back of love.' I still don't know what he meant by that and I'm not sure he does either, but it shut the rest of them up.

We were putting the finishing touches to the mix when Bill came down to hear it. He listened to what we'd done and he said, 'This is fucking terrible.' He turned to me and said, 'What have you done to this song?' To be fair to him, he was unprepared for how radically we'd changed it. It wasn't what he was expecting at all. Mac was furious about the criticism and pretty much threw him out of the studio. We then continued to work as we had been before, as if Bill hadn't been there. We just knew that what we had done was good and that we were on the right track. It wouldn't have occurred to us to try to do something different.

A couple of days later, we heard that Bill, after listening to the recording a few times, now totally got it. He had changed his position to 'This is the best record since "Anarchy in the UK".' Some turnaround!

Despite Bill's change of heart, I was still in hot water, and the record company saw me as the villain of the piece. Their vision for the song was something entirely different. All this friction became a big emotional thing for me. The idea that the record company was angry with me was very disappointing, and I worried that I might never get the chance to produce anything ever again.

We moved on to the initial rehearsals for *Porcupine*, which proved a bit problematic. Some of the relationships in the band were becoming a little frosty. The way they had worked in the past was that all the songs so far had been created in a rehearsal room, rather than written earlier, and there was a rule that no one was allowed to tell anyone else what to do. That had worked at the start, but no one really wanted to suggest much when they knew that it was going to be shot down in flames for no other reason than grumpiness and inter-band squabbles. We ended up spending days on very long and largely fruitless jam sessions. At this point Bill had another of his ideas. He said, 'I'm going to book you on a string of little gigs around the north of Scotland. There will be no road crew, no roadies, just you all in a van, unable to get away from each other for a few weeks. It will be the making of you. It should just be the five of you. Ian can do the mix, and also play guitar.'

In the early days of the band, Mac had played a lot of guitar, but by then he was starting to come into his own as a singer and frontman. He didn't want to play guitar as much any more, so I sometimes played some of the parts for him. The idea that I could do that and also do the mix at the same time, though, was totally mad, and I said as much to Bill. He was adamant, however, so we drove up to Scotland, where Bill had booked all these gigs in tiny little venues and church halls and weird places like Aviemore Ski Resort. The Bunnymen could have filled quite big venues in England by then, but the idea was that hardly anyone would see these gigs. No one would review them, so there would be no pressure from that direction. I guess it was Bill's idea of a bonding session, as well as a press-worthy stunt.

Bill Drummond came up to Scotland for at least one of the gigs. We started playing and I have a vivid memory of looking to the side and seeing him there, sitting on the side of the stage. The odd thing was that he was dressed as a comedy Frenchman. He was wearing a striped T-shirt and he had a beret on. A red napkin was tucked into his stripy shirt and he was eating a baguette. The baguette was absolutely massive. There weren't many baguettes around in those days, so this was very unusual – you couldn't just nip into ASDA and pick up a baguette like you can now. Retrospectively, I think this might have been a dream that I have somehow turned into a memory.

7

'THE CUTTER'

'The Back of Love' was released as an early single for the as yet unrecorded album, and to everyone's delight it entered the top twenty – a milestone for the band. With that, came their first *Top of the Pops* appearance, which felt like a really big deal. I was lucky enough to go to the filming, which in those days was in Shepherd's Bush. There I bumped into Bryan Ferry, who I hadn't seen since Original Mirrors accompanied them on their European Tour.

The success of that track really centred Warner Brothers' attention on the Bunnymen. Although they were still unconvinced by my credentials, they cautiously agreed to let me go with the band to Rockfield Studios to start work on their album.

It's always a pleasure, arriving at Rockfield, surrounded by green hills and boasting a full fridge of food and some peace and quiet, in which bands could really focus. Although, honestly, I wasn't sure that we had that much to focus on, as there really weren't many songs written. What we did have was a set of loosely formed ideas and jams that we hoped would evolve into something special – and off we went.

Seeing as I was Kingbird at that time, Mac could become Ian, which is how I've known him ever since. We got a few tracks down, and then we started on vocals. Ian didn't have too many words prepared and liked to write as we recorded. We had a routine of starting late into the night, and our inhibitions would drop away with cocktails of hot chocolate and brandy. As the night wore on, Ian would sometimes astonish me with his singing and words, which blended with Will's imaginative and inspired guitar playing, all sitting on top of the magnificent rhythm section and beats by the astonishing Pete de Freitas. It was exciting to be around.

Eventually we had rough mixes of the tracks, and in the cold light of day we had managed to transition the jam sessions into songs, but now that they existed I could get a new perspective on them. It was obvious that we needed to take them to a more magical place and hone the arrangements. This meant re-recording, and a conversation with the record company.

It seemed to me at that time that I had stiff competition, and that some very notable people now wanted to produce the Bunnymen, from Robert Plant to Steve Lillywhite. Korova felt that maybe it was time for a change. It still amazes me the faith that Will, Ian and the rest of the band had in me. Even against this backdrop, they were adamant that they wanted to keep recording with me. This faith gave me my start, and it was more faith than I had in myself, probably. This was a pivotal moment for them, and their future careers possibly depended on it, so it was no small decision. Yet they kept that faith. To this day, it's something that I'm terribly grateful for.

This left Bill with the tricky task of convincing the record company. He fixed this in a very Bill Drummond way: he simply told the label that someone else would produce the album. Then we carried on as normal, in Townhouse Studios. Bill always operated by the seat of his pants, and although this was exciting, it meant that you never really quite knew what was going on, and of course the events leading up to the session, and the subterfuge involved, piled a lot of pressure on me. I felt like I had to absolutely prove myself, and give it everything I'd got, whether that meant producing, playing guitar, changing arrangements or rewriting sections. I wouldn't let anything come between me and the outcome that I felt

I had to achieve. The Bunnymen's third album *Porcupine* was as much a pivotal moment for them as 'Rescue' had been earlier. 'The Back of Love' had gone top twenty and got them on *Top of the Pops* for the first time, so they were poised to make the leap. They just needed something that could follow that and build on it. Even though 'The Cutter' in its original form wasn't an obvious single, we all felt it could be something special, and that's why we put so much effort into developing it.

In my mind, the song took such a crazy significance that it was almost as if my future depended on it. I needed to get that song right whatever it took. What if I never had an opportunity like that again? I can't tell you how stressful it was. A guitar line here or a middle eight there mattered so, so much to me. Every single note had to be right and I thought about nothing else. But the Bunnymen, and Ian in particular, showed so much belief in me at that vital point that I just couldn't fail.

While we were working on 'The Cutter', the flat that Will and I shared in Liverpool was broken into, and someone would have to go back to sort this out so that the session could continue. Will went back to Liverpool and I carried on recording. Ian wanted to finish the song, so he asked me to play some guitars. He directed me, saying, 'When I sing "Spare us the cutter," can you make a guitar sound like a scythe?' Having never heard a scythe and being completely ignorant of what one might sound like, I set up some effects and came up with an idea to strike the guitar very hard into reverb and tremolo, while frantically wriggling the whammy bar on my Gretsch Tennessean guitar. It all added up to a very beautiful – but at the same time very dramatic – guitar effect. I guess it could have been the sound of some form of imaginary glorious scythe, and I kind of knew that this was what Ian was after.

Then I added some piano lines to the new middle eight that we'd come up with, which would later be secretly doubled on synthesiser by Messrs Balfe and Drummond, to magical effect.

We decamped back to Amazon Studios in Liverpool to do vocals and a few overdubs. Unexpectedly, Bill decided that it would be great to enlist an Indian violinist called Shankar to play on the album, and he came up to Liverpool to record with us. I don't know how Bill found him, but he's gone on to an illustrious career, playing with Elton John, Sting, Bruce Springsteen, Frank Zappa and tons of others. I thought 'The Cutter' might be a good place to start, as it needed an intro.

The way Shankar worked was that he had a girl with him whose job seemed to be rolling up spliffs. He'd go into the studio and say, 'First, could you please turn the lights down,' and while we got the lights how he liked them, this girl would roll a ginormous spliff. Halfway through the spliff, he'd say, 'Roll the tape!', and he'd just solo endlessly, playing all this psychedelic stuff with heavy echo. It totally obliterated the rest of the song, and to make it fit was like wading through treacle.

Will and I turned to each other and agreed that this wasn't going to work as an intro. We both thought of the introduction to 'Matthew and Son' by Cat Stevens. I'd been playing that over and over in the flat, so it was fresh in our minds. I felt it was a perfect intro, and I was fascinated by some of the reverb sounds they'd used on that record. I said to Shankar, 'Look, we need something for the beginning of the song. Can you play an intro? Something immediate, something that everyone will love?' He said, 'Like what?' As a suggestion I sang him the opening motif to 'Matthew and Son' and he responded by playing it back at me, in a vaguely recognisable way, but with a sliding Indian lilt, and it sounded so great. It was exactly what we needed. That became the opening to 'The Cutter'. So if you ever hear the beginning of that record and think that it sounds like 'Matthew and Son', that's the reason.

That evening, Ian added the vocals to the middle eight. Out of the blue, he came up with the words and melodies that took the song from pretty good to euphoric. It was so unexpected and moving that I was stunned. It was awesome, and I played it over and over again. We'd nailed it.

It was a difficult record to make and there were a lot of crises to overcome during the process. The songs underwent many changes of direction. There was the looser, less refined first version at Rockfield, all the adventures with Shankar, and the re-recordings needed to enable the evolution from jam sessions to songs. It took a lot out of us all, but it doesn't matter how you get there – what matters is that you do.

The track was then mixed, unbeknown to us, by Dave Balfe and Bill Drummond. They took Will's guitars off, featured the ones that I'd played, and doubled my piano line on a synth. Later, they told us that it was trumpets because for some reason they thought we wouldn't be as mad if they had added trumpets. It clearly wasn't trumpets, though – it was obviously a synth. We were all really annoyed when we found out what they'd done, but, looking back, this was now the best version. It feels like it couldn't have been any other way. I think it was the standout track on the album and it became the Bunnymen's highest-charting single. It's lived long in the memory, and I still hear it on the radio, and it sounds great to this day.

Not long after the album, I got a call from Bill asking if I would join the band and become a fifth member, probably because we had been working so closely for the past year. This was such a massive temptation. I adored the band, and they were my friends, but I couldn't shake the feeling that when the four of them played together there was a unique chemistry that I treasured. With me as a member of the band, I knew that would be altered. If I had tried to slot into that format, more would have been lost than gained. So, with a heavy heart, I decided not to accept the offer.

Ironically, the next time I saw them, far from it being just the four individuals, they had been joined by a lot of other people onstage. They had this guy Mike playing the rhythm guitar, Jake the roadie was on keyboards, Tim Whittaker was on bongos, there was someone on the cello – and all these new musicians were now part of the band. So perhaps I made the wrong choice. So much for preserving the chemistry!

8

'JEAN'S NOT HAPPENING'

The Bunnymen were signed to a label called Korova, which was part of Warner Brothers group and run by Rob Dickins. I had a history with Rob from the Big in Japan days, when he ran Warner Bros Publishing. He had taken the band into the studio and produced and paid for some Big in Japan recordings.

Other than BBC Maida Vale studios, where I had recorded a John Peel session, it was probably my first experience in a supposed state-of-the-art London recording studio. In reality, it was a pretty shady place in Fulham under a used-car lot, and my fondest memory is of the six-foot-plus and rather large-framed house engineer Alan Winstanley having to keep kicking the tape machine to get it working.

When I moved to London after the band split up, Rob signed me to Warner Bros Publishing – my first publishing contract. They were based off Oxford Street in Berners Street and had a small demo studio set up in the back room. Surprisingly, he gave me the keys to the back entrance in Berners Mews and told me I could let myself in after everyone had left for the day and use the studio to become better at recording and writing songs.

Those were exciting times for me. I took Rob up on his offer and would spend long nights in the empty office doing just that. I was learning and perfecting my craft without the pressure of time constraints or funding worries. Looking back, it was an amazing gesture and showed a lot of faith on Rob's behalf.

Echo & the Bunnymen had given me a legacy of sorts. The *Porcupine* album had been a great success and I was now seen as a producer. As a result, I was approached by Michael Head, more commonly known as Mick, and Chris McCaffrey, who we used to call 'Biffa'. They had a group called the Pale Fountains. When I first noticed them, they used to walk around Liverpool in sandals and shorts, looking like a cross between Haircut 100 and the Famous Five.

Mick and Biffa had done an indie single on the independent Belgian label Les Disques du Crépuscule that I really liked. It was called '(There's Always) Something on

My Mind' and it sounded like a 1960s movie soundtrack – Astrud Gilberto meets Carlos Jobim on a sunny day. This was a strange concoction for the early 1980s, and it piqued my interest. They were now signed to Virgin Records but were disappointed by the lack of reaction to their first album and had returned to Liverpool to regroup.

After a couple of meetings, I found that I really enjoyed chatting with them. Mick was the guy who wrote the songs while Biffa had more of a sense of the direction they should take, but I wasn't sold on their Burt Bacharach fixation. I adore Bacharach, of course, but I felt maybe we could have come up with a harder-edged approach and find a different vision. The band Love was a big deal for me, and on that train of thought I mentioned to them the Love cover of Bacharach's 'My Little Red Book'. I suggested that instead of sounding like Burt Bacharach, we should try to make a record that sounded like Love covering Burt Bacharach. They reacted really positively to this idea and it became our loose plan of action for the album.

I don't recall exactly how, but we ended up marooned in a studio somewhere north of Inverness, near Culloden. It really was in the middle of nowhere. We began recording . . . *From Across the Kitchen Table* and I threw myself into this wholeheartedly, but the boundary between producer and artist were very blurred to me. Because I was writing all the string parts and arranging the tunes, while at the same time coaching Mick's younger brother John – at that time a fledgling guitarist destined to be a maestro – I probably allowed myself to become too emotionally involved. I'd drifted into a place where I was almost co-writing rather than just producing, particularly on a track called 'Jean's Not Happening'.

In the studio, the obsessive focus on the music, which was part of my nature, often came to the fore. If I'm working on a track and it's not right to my ears, I can feel physically sick. It's a horrible thing and the only way to deal with it is to keep working until the song is right. It's ridiculous and it drives me nuts, but I have to pursue the direction in which I think the song is leading us, because for me the song is king, and a good song will always tell you where it wants to go, if you listen.

Once, my friend Rob asked me to play a song at his fiftieth birthday celebration. It should have been a relaxed pleasure in the open air among friends. The band leader was the brilliant Nick Heyward and they had prepared 'Sense', which is a relatively simple song of mine. We sound checked and instead of just singing along karaoke-style, my mind focused on the incorrect minor details. The usual frustrating obsessive symptoms appeared and had me under a spell, and I must have made those poor guys play the song fifty times.

Everyone in the hotel trying to relax was being driven mad by the repetition. It was embarrassing. My friends teased me so mercilessly about it that it became the catalyst to me letting go of that behaviour. After this, my obsessive bent was finally brought under control, and I could finally relax, be comfortable, and be in the moment onstage. I still shudder to think about it, though. I have mellowed over the years and, with hindsight, I should have learnt to keep my distance earlier.

When Virgin heard the album, they felt that it should sound more contemporary, and to that end they brought in someone new to mix it in a more modern style. Nowadays that isn't such a big deal – new producers are brought in all the time – but back then, I felt let down because I'd put so much of myself into that record and it was being snatched from me. I thought we were all in the trenches together, but the band didn't really fight for the vision we shared. It was a harsh lesson. It was the first time that anything like this had ever happened to me and I wasn't prepared for it.

Afterwards, I shared a flat with Biffa, and we all remained friends. I came to realise that . . . *From Across the Kitchen Table* wasn't my record; it was theirs and not mine to control. I was just the producer. People often think that musicians must be hurt if they release music and it's not a hit, but I don't think that's always the case. Whether it's a hit or not is down to a million things that you have no control over. There's not a lot you can do about it. It's the things that you *do* control that matter to you. Those are the things that can really wound you.

As the '80s progressed, I was drifting further and further into the role of the record producer and further and further away from the songwriter and guitarist I wanted to be. I hadn't set out to become a producer, and I only really did it because I thought Echo & the Bunnymen were so great and I loved being around them. And from there I just naturally fell into working with other people on their records. In a sense it was flattering and a positive, but it kind of deflected me from writing my own songs for about ten years.

The Pale Fountains' album crystalised the thought that, at this time in my life, I shouldn't be a producer. I wanted something that was mine, although I carried on working as a producer for a while and a lot of it was fun. I had a great time and creatively I learnt a lot from the musicians I worked with, which proved invaluable in the years to come. Also, I didn't see many other options. I wasn't in a band and I wasn't quite ready to put my money where my mouth was.

9

'IT'S MAD UP THERE'

During this period in the mid-'80s, I was so preoccupied with music, and so focused on the work I was doing with bands in the studio, that it took me a long time to realise the extent to which my flat was riddled with ghosts.

Sharing a flat with Will had been great, but eventually he decided to move in with his girlfriend. I got a new flat on the third floor of a Georgian terraced house in Hope Street, Liverpool, which also came with an attic room above. Paul Simpson from the Wild Swans lived on the ground floor and Julian Cope's ex-wife Kathy was in between us, so socially it was a great place to live. Hope Street itself is a really interesting part of town. It has two cathedrals, one at each end, and between them is the Everyman Theatre and the Philharmonic Hall. There's a lot going on and a lot of strange history linked to it, and it's only a short walk down the hill to the centre of town.

For the longest time after I moved in, I didn't consciously recognise that anything was odd about the place. I'd be sitting in the living room at night and these strange dragging and clanking noises would be coming from the attic room above. There would be sudden bangs, so loud they'd make you jump. I told myself that the noises couldn't be coming from upstairs, as there was no one up there. They must have been coming from next door. This seemed reasonable because the guy next door was pretty weird. He had a CB radio and sometimes his broadcasts would come through our speakers. I'd be trying to listen to music when, all of a sudden, this harsh staticky trucker speak would break through. If anyone was going to be banging stuff in the middle of the night, I thought, it would have been him. I asked him to keep the noise down when I saw him, but he seemed unimpressed by this. He acted like he wasn't doing anything wrong and flat out denied making banging noises at night.

I was producing the Pale Fountains' album at the time. Mick Head would be round the flat a lot and would often crash over. He'd go up the stairs to sleep in the attic room at night, but when I got up in the morning, he was always back on the sofa in the living room. This happened with other people as well. I didn't really think anything of it at the time. After I had been in there a little while, my girlfriend Becky moved in with me. She was nowhere near as blind or as preoccupied as I was. She'd say, 'Ian, there's something very weird about this place,' but I didn't really listen and I just told her that it was next door. Biffa lived with us for a while as well and in theory the attic was his bedroom, but he wouldn't stay in there. He was going out with Jayne Casey at the time and she was round a lot. Pretty quickly they moved in together, which left just me and Becky.

One night we were woken by a massive explosion. I ran to the window and looked out to my right at the house next door, and there was this jet of flames pouring out of the window. The heat that came off it was unbelievable. People were shouting, 'Get out! Get out of the house!', so we both legged it out. For some reason there was a sofa on the pavement opposite. We spent much of the night sat on that sofa watching the house burn while the fire brigade and the police ran about. It turned out that there had been a gas explosion caused by next door's cooker. Their house was gutted and burnt out, but fortunately the fire brigade was able to get the blaze under control quite quickly and our flat remained intact. One wall was warped by the heat, but it was otherwise okay. What this meant was that, with an empty shell next door, we could no longer pretend that the strange banging and dragging noises were coming from there. We had to accept that they were coming from the attic.

Things started to get weirder. If you put something on the bed and left the room, then it might have moved when you returned, or have vanished completely. One time we came back and found a load of things from the kitchen piled up on the bed. The dragging noises would come every night and sometimes there were terrible smells in the attic. I can't really describe what the smells were like because I've never come across anything like them, before or after. One time I tried to go up there and I physically couldn't get into the room because the smell was like a thick wall that I couldn't get past. After Biffa moved out, I set up my tape recorder up there. In theory I was going to use it as a studio, but I just couldn't bring myself to work in there. I was too scared to be in that room by myself for any length of time. We asked Mick and other people who had stayed over why we always found them back on the sofa in the morning, but none of them wanted to talk about it. Mick would just say, 'It's mad up there,' but he wouldn't explain any further.

The woman who lived in the basement flat, Sharon, told us that she'd heard there were a couple of underground passages from the Anglican cathedral to those houses. These had been used by body snatchers in the nineteenth century when they were taking body parts from the cemetery. Becky found an article on the internet recently that backed a lot of this up. What happened was that, in 1826, the dockers working down George's Dock got suspicious about the smell coming from three barrels, which were due to be shipped up to the Leith Docks near Edinburgh. The barrels were opened and found to be full of naked dead bodies, with three or four adult corpses squashed into each barrel. This was the era of body snatchers, when people would dig up corpses and sell them to medical schools for anatomical study. Body snatchers were known at the time as 'resurrection men'. Between 1827 and 1828, William Burke and William Hare in Scotland famously started killing people to sell their bodies to Dr Robert Knox, an influential lecturer in the anatomy department at the University of Edinburgh, so there was clearly quite a sizeable market for corpses.

The barrels were traced to 8 Hope Street. The house numbers have changed since then, but this was our neighbour's house. People had been complaining about the smell coming from the basement, but the man who was renting it told everyone it was because he was a cooper trading in fish oil. The police raided the basement and what they found down there sounds like pure horror. In total, there were twenty-two decaying bodies and sacks and barrels in varying stages of being filled with these corpses. There was one barrel filled with brine. When that was emptied, they found the bodies of many babies at the bottom.

The bodies, as Sharon told it, had been stolen from St James' Cemetery. This was further along Hope Street and is now the land where the Anglican cathedral stands. Before it became a cemetery in the nineteenth century, it was a stone quarry and there are a bunch of tunnels coming from it, some of which are blocked off. According to newspaper reports at the time, though, the bodies were thought to come from the workhouse which stood at the other end of Hope Street, where the Catholic cathedral now stands.

Whether all this explains why our attic was the focus of all the strangeness, I don't know. Eventually, me and Becky had enough and moved out. The people who moved in after us had the same problems with bangs and noises and things moving about. They had a cat that used to sit at the bottom of the attic stairs, where the noises came from. It would never go up there, but it used to sit in the same place all night, looking up the stairs with its fur up on his back. Sometimes it would make horrible noises, like hissing or snarling. They moved out almost immediately.

I know that a lot of people will read this and think, 'That's nonsense. There's no such thing as ghosts.' All I can say is: you wouldn't think that if you had lived in that flat.

10

'MY BOYISH DAYS'

Going back to Liverpool after I left Original Mirrors felt quite cathartic. I was among my friends again. Everyone was a couple of years older and they had progressed further along their paths, but I still felt comfortable with them. All the time I was producing, I was also looking around, searching for the right people to form a band with. One of the things that I've been searching for my entire life is the right frontman or frontwoman – I've always felt that I've never found the Jagger to my Richards. This is what would lead to me having to sing my own songs in the Lightning Seeds, with all the inner struggles I had doing that. For a short period after returning to Liverpool, however, I thought I'd found the right person. This was

Paul Simpson, previously of the Teardrop Explodes and the Wild Swans.

I knew Paul from Eric's, where he was famous for wearing enormously baggy tweed trousers. They were inspired by David Bowie, those trousers, but there was also a '50s English-gentleman edge to his image. He had floppy hair and you'd see him marching up and down Bold Street in this get-up. He was too cool for school, really. He was poetic and sensitive, and he looked great. Paul was a mate of Will's and he shared a flat with Pete de Freitas. Pete had produced a Wild Swans single called 'Revolutionary Spirit' (1982), which I really liked, at a time when I didn't like much else.

Paul had one of those romantic epic voices that you used to get in the New Wave era – voices that went really well with the cold, harsh, synthetic sounds of the early electronic instruments. Steve, the singer in Original Mirrors, had a good voice technically, but it didn't move my heart emotionally in any way. This really confused me when I was in that band. I knew that he was a really good singer but his voice just didn't move me and I just couldn't solve that conundrum in my head at that time. Steve didn't have whatever quality it is that makes you want to listen to someone. Paul, on the other hand, had that in spades. It didn't come easily, but when he sang it felt like it mattered. The song 'Revolutionary Spirit' is a great example of that.

The Wild Swans had done that first great single, but I don't think they had done much else at that time. They seemed to be drifting and they weren't putting in the hard work that you needed to if you were going to make something of a band. I thought that if Paul and I started working together then we could really do something wonderful, so we formed a band called Care.

Care, of course, was a terrible name for a band. For one thing, it sounded too much like the Cure. What happened was that me and Paul, along with Bill Drummond and David Balfe, who were publishing our songs, sat down and came up with a list of band names. It must have been the worst list of potential band names that anyone had ever put together. Perhaps that was a sign. We chose Care from the list because it was the best of a bad bunch. Perhaps if we had waited a little longer, we might have come up with something better.

Very quickly, we got a record deal with Arista Records. The guy at Arista, Simon, was a big fan of Paul's. He was excited to work with us and prepared to give us major label backing to make a record. The first thing we recorded was a song called 'My Boyish Days'. This started off as an old tune of mine that I'd had kicking around for a while. Paul threw away my lyrics and wrote something much better. This was exactly what I had been looking for and exactly what I needed. It seemed to me that Paul's voice and lyrics were everything that I had been missing. He came up with some lovely, great words.

Arista put us in a studio with a producer to record the song, but I didn't think that the results were very good. It was a better song than it was a recording and I much preferred the demo that I'd done before. So, me being me, I decided to be our producer. I had certain ideas about how things should sound and when someone else produced us, the result was not the sound that I had in my head. It was not what I believed the song should sound like, for better or worse. It's not that I thought I was great and that I was the only one good enough to do it, more I thought the song wanted to be a certain thing and if we didn't capture that then we were letting it down.

Our next single was called 'Flaming Sword' and I decided that I was going to produce it. Pete from the Bunnymen came in to play the drums, while I played everything else. It was an early version of the Lightning Seeds in that respect – it had my melody and production but married to Paul's voice and words. It wasn't a hit, but it skirted around the chart and got a bit of attention. I remember we were staying in the Columbia hotel in London and Holly Johnson came over to visit. The first Frankie Goes to Hollywood single, 'Relax', had been out a while but was still hovering outside the top fifty during the final months of 1983. 'Flaming Sword' was at a similar place in the charts, but ours had gone up a few places while Holly's single had dropped down a bit. This was just before the BBC banned 'Relax' and Frankie became this insane phenomenon, while the Care single disappeared without trace. That all seems inevitable with hindsight, but I can still remember the pair of us sitting in this hotel and neither of us had any idea of what was about to happen. We were talking about how our singles were doing in this really innocent way.

'Flaming Sword' did enough to convince Arista to send me and Paul into the studio to record an album, which was something that I'd never done before as an artist. The single had had enough of an identity to help establish who we were, so it was a good start. I had this idea that I wanted to make psychedelic pop music using a lot of orchestral instruments. So I hired cello players, strings and piccolos and that kind of thing, and I set about trying to capture the songs as I heard them in my head. A lot of what the Lightning Seeds became was a home-made bedroom version of the sort of stuff I was doing in Care, but without the money and without Paul's voice or words.

Focusing deeply on the work as I did, I failed to notice the extent to which Paul hated what it was that I was doing. We were strange bedfellows in a way because I was all about music and he was more about the aesthetic of it. He was quite sensitive whereas when I was in the studio, I was very driven – I could be quite a force of nature in terms of getting things how I wanted them. Paul felt he couldn't express himself properly when I was like that and that I wasn't hearing what he was saying.

About two-thirds of the way through the album, Paul wrote me a letter saying that he didn't want to do it anymore. I've still got that letter – it's five pages long and written in pink ink, and what he says in it is basically true. He said that he was writing to me instead of talking to me because I would have just talked him round. I would have tried to convince him that what we were doing was good and that he was just a bit depressed. He said that the communication between us had gradually degenerated and that when we spoke face to face, he was always trying to bite his tongue to reduce friction and argument. He said he hated the album and he hated what we were doing; there was not one thing he liked about it. Every step we took was 'doomed to failure', he wrote. It was quite a dramatic letter, but that doesn't mean he was wrong.

He wrote that his contribution had gone down from 50 to 5 per cent. That was one thing I'm not sure I agree with, because if you listen to the album now, his voice, his lyrics and his personality are very strong and present. The rest of what he was saying, though, was spot on. He said that I was not the easiest person in the world to work with and that I tended to dominate the conversation. He felt he couldn't stand up to me even on a minor point. It got to the stage where just the sight of a recording studio gave him a sore throat. He wrote that, 'Although it's quite a likeable sort of thrashing, it is frustrating and I don't feel I'm expressing myself.' In hindsight, *A Likeable Sort of Thrashing* would have been a great name for the album.

Now, I've always seen myself as being a bit hidden or inconsequential. I was the guy who stood off to one side, the outsider, who never really fitted in and who was scared to stand out. What Paul's letter shows is that there was something about being in a studio and working with musicians that changed me. In that world, I came to life. That was my comfortable environment. When I'm with a group of musicians in a room I feel secure enough to become quite single-minded. It's as if all the parts of my personality that are normally lacking are suddenly present. They are maybe *too* present, perhaps as if to overcompensate for not being around when I need them normally.

After the Lightning Seeds achieved some success in the '90s, someone released all the Care recordings as an album called *Diamonds and Emeralds* (1997). There's a lot of unfinished stuff on there, but you can hear what we were going for. The cover art seems to sum up the problems we had in the band. You would expect it to be a photo of Paul, look-ing all elegant and handsome like a real pin-up pop star. Maybe I would have been lurking in the background some-where, like Chris Lowe from the Pet Shop Boys. Instead, I'm right at the front of the photo, staring down the lens, a blue sky and fluttering bright kites above me. Paul, on the other hand, is in black and white and in the background. He's wearing a jacket with a wide-collared white shirt and his good trousers, but he's slumped in a hedge by the side of the road, staring at me with a look of either bemusement or horror.

Being in a studio for me was often a desperate fight to get on tape what I heard in my head, and sometimes anyone who gets in the way of this can become a bit of a casualty. I think that's what happened with Paul – I think I basically ran him over. I don't think it was arrogance; it was more about certainty. This need to capture on tape what you hear in your head is one of the things that a lot of people don't get about musicians. It's every bit as much of a compulsion as drugs or gambling. I used to wonder if I was on the autis-tic spectrum because of the extent to which that aspect of myself would take precedence over everything else. I don't think that now. It has eased off over the years and I have it much more under control, which I now know isn't how autism works.

And this absolute certainty is something that I recognise in other artists. To be in a band and make music takes a kind of toughness. Someone who goes to a strange town where they don't know anyone and gets up on stage will know the battles that they have to fight to keep doing that, night after night. For me, my toughness comes from a belief in my songs. I've surprised myself at how willing I've been to fight for them and not back down. I'm not a brave person in my normal life, but I can be brave with my work in the studio, just because of that certainty about the sound in my head. I think a musician needs to reach that place where you won't take no for an answer because you're going to need to take that strength with you out into the world and onto the stage.

In some ways, Paul may have found it hard to leave his comfort zone and be up for that fight. Looking back, I feel like he might have lacked the level of mental toughness and pragmatism that you need in the music industry. I'm not saying that's a negative thing – it's probably a plus, person-ality wise. I liked Paul all the way through all this, before, during and after the band. We've done stuff together since. After he had reformed the Wild Swans, for example, I pro-duced their *Space Flower* (1990) album. But when I think of the musicians I've known who have gone out and forged their own musical path – people like Holly Johnson, Terry

Hall or Ian McCulloch, say – they all have a certain prag-matism and a certain toughness. They know how to argue back; they don't put up with bullshit. People like that fight like hell with me in the studio and sometimes they'll win and sometimes I'll win. In the end, it's usually the record that wins.

The collapse of Care, with hindsight, turned out to be the last of my attempts to form a band with other people. Other than putting my own stuff out under the name the Lightning Seeds, I've not joined or tried to form a band since. I always felt that I shouldn't be the singer in the Lightning Seeds and that's something that has never left me. Of course I'm happy with my career and the Light-ning Seeds' music, but I do feel that in another world and in a different dimension, if there was a different singer that came along, who knows what might have happened. I'm aware that the only Lightning Seeds song to go to number one in the UK charts was 'Three Lions' (1996), which was a track featuring other singers.

Paul had all the qualities that I needed, but those qualities, it turned out, were the same ones that made a person unable to work with me. This was something of an unsolvable conundrum. I think deep down I just lacked the belief that I had what it took in terms of voice, charisma and presence to be at the front of a band, so I went back to producing for a while.

I didn't know then that what I was waiting for wasn't the right singer – it was the right song. When I wrote a song good enough, my belief in it would mean that I would have no choice but to walk out on that stage by myself and sing.

11

WARM ASPIRATIONS IN THE USA

In 1986, shortly after my adventures with Paul and Care, I was hired by an American band called the Three O'Clock to produce their next record. This was my first production challenge where I'd been approached by someone I didn't know, solely based on my reputation.

The Three O'Clock were part of the American Paisley Underground scene that gave us bands like R.E.M. and the Bangles, and they were big fans of the Bunnymen album I produced. They had signed to I.R.S. Records, who had a lot of success with R.E.M., the Go-Go's and Belinda Carlisle. I'd never been to America before, so the thought of jetting off to Los Angeles – and being paid to do so – was quite a buzz.

In the lead-up, I had a call from their manager, John. He was a great guy who was a big fan of the whole Liverpool scene. He had visited the New Manx hotel in Liverpool when he was a student solely based on the fact that the Teardrop Explodes had lived there. This was in the days before the internet of course, so there was not much communication between us beforehand. I told him I'd come if I could bring Becky and my own engineer, a guy called Pete, because it's important for a producer to have an engineer they know and work well with. He agreed, so the three of us got on a plane and flew to California. It felt like a great adventure.

When we landed in Los Angeles, Becky and I went through Customs and waited for Pete to emerge. He didn't appear. After we had waited for the best part of an hour, we were told that he had gone back to England. He hadn't been allowed into the country and had been put on a plane back home. To this day I still don't know why that was – we asked Pete later, but he didn't want to talk about it. So we arrived without our engineer, in this strange big country that we really knew nothing about, which put me in a bit of a tricky spot. I was nervous beforehand and this helped keep me unsettled.

Looking back, it's funny how naive we were about Los Angeles and how you're supposed to act there. We didn't realise that you had to drive everywhere and that walking was just impossible. Shortly after we arrived, we went to a supermarket and our mouths dropped open. We'd never really seen anything like it before – it was like a city; it just went on and on. As we entered the pharmacy next door to the supermarket, a bunch of jeeps pulled up outside and a dozen or so really big, frightening guys got out and headed towards us.

Back in England, I'd read a lot about all the gangs in LA. They had sounded terrifying. There were reports of seemingly constant drive-by shootings and people getting caught in the middle of inter-gang warfare. I had been a bit nervous about going to America in the first place, so when I saw all these scary guys coming towards the pharmacy, my immediate thought was, 'Oh no, it's one of the gangs I've read about!' They looked even more dangerous than I'd imagined. They were wearing bear skins and chain mail, and they had huge arms like bodybuilders. Some of them had helmets on, as if they were Vikings. They were all way over six feet tall. I was still jet-lagged and confused, so it was a lot to deal with.

This squad of terrifying heavies entered the shop. I said to Becky, 'It's one of them gangs! We're in trouble. Let's hide in the back of the shop.' We got as far back from them as we could and hid. Every now and again, I'd peep around the side of the aisle to see what was happening. Oddly, the barbarians were just milling around and chatting. One of them was buying shampoo.

A shop assistant approached us and asked if we were okay. I said to her in a hissed whisper, 'It's that gang. We're trying to stay out of the way because they look dangerous.' She turned round, looked at those fierce guys by the tills, and then looked down at me hiding at the back of the shop. Then she said, 'Right behind this building is the film studio lot. They're filming *Conan the Barbarian* at the moment.' With that, she smiled and walked off and left us to it. That was my first afternoon in LA. I really wasn't covering myself in glory.

Still, we settled in and I got stuck into the recording of the record, which went well. It was the first production job that I'd done that wasn't with a Liverpool band or people I vaguely knew, so despite all my reservations about being a producer, I did enjoy myself. I got on really well with John Silva and the band's drummer, Danny Benair, both of whom I still consider great friends. Becky and I had an apartment in Burbank and I loved being in LA. I loved all the Mexican street food and the local club scene and the whole vibe. Just being there and making music was a real thrill.

We started recording in a studio in Griffith Park in the Santa Monica Mountains. This is the place where they shot some key scenes in *Rebel Without a Cause*. It's been in loads of movies and TV shows since, but it was the fact that it was in *Rebel Without a Cause* that blew my mind and made it seem especially iconic. It's not far from the Hollywood sign and it's high up, so you can see Los Angeles spreading out for miles and miles up there. The studio belonged to a jazz musician called Chick Corea, and downstairs in the studio there were desks and desks of women all talking on the telephone. I asked what they were doing and was told that Chick was a big figure in a new religion and he had set up a call centre to help promote it. The idea that there could be new religions seemed crazy to me at the time, and this was another of the things that marked out LA as this extraordinary place. Being there was quite an education and there was a lot to take in. Even getting used to the constant sunshine took me a while, although it meant that my habit of always wearing sunglasses was suddenly entirely normal, rather than some strange affectation. Chick's religion was Scientology, it turned out, although I'd never heard of it at the time.

When we came to mix the album, we went to a studio in Reno because we were pretty tight on budget and their manager, John, had found this place that seemed very cost-effective. Reno is over the California border in Nevada and it was quite something to see the effect that this had on all the Americans. Gambling is legal in Nevada and Reno is like a poor man's Vegas. To Americans at that time, being somewhere that you could gamble was a massive deal. We all arrived in Reno and the first thing the band did was to go to a casino and lose all their money. That was the first night. They lost everything and had no money for food or anything. They were in tears about it. It was the speed of it that amazed me – the very moment they physically could gamble, they did. I don't think they could have thrown their money away any quicker if they had tried. There were no regular hotels in Reno and you essentially have to stay in rooms in casinos, so you were never really far away from temptation.

We went into this studio and because I'd been told it was so cheap, I was a little nervous about what sort of equipment they would have and how good it would be. I was amazed when I saw it, though. They had all the latest top-of-the-line gear. The odd thing was that a lot of the equipment they had wasn't plugged in and had never been used. When I asked the people there about it, they had no clue how it worked. I slowly realised that no one there really knew what they were doing. The guy told me that we were the first proper session that they had ever booked in. 'Oh, have you just opened?' I asked. He said no. He told me that the people who owned the studio were a little shady and that the studio was a conduit they channelled money through. The only thing that the studio had been used for was as a venue for parties thrown by one of their wives. So the studio was stuffed with all this wonderful equipment, but it was only really there as a very elaborate backdrop.

That was my first taste of America. What with the Scientology call centre, the barbarian gangs of movie extras, the dodgy Reno studio and Pete being refused entry, I feel that I got the full LA experience. By anyone's standards, that was a proper first trip to the US.

12

'A GREAT BUNCH OF LADS'

Rockfield Studios is a recording studio in Monmouthshire, Wales. It was one of the first residential studios in the world, more by necessity than anything else. Because there was nowhere even remotely close for bands to stay, they had to provide accommodation at the studio. When you are at Rockfield you are out in the country, away from the rest of the world, with no distraction from the music you are making. It feels very secluded, especially if you are a lad from Liverpool. There are no shops around, no local amenities, just fields for miles and miles in all directions.

I was booked to do a session with Pete Wylie and told to go down a day before the session was supposed to start. Pete was going to get there the next day. Rockfield offered special producer's accommodation. It was basically an old Welsh farm, so it was hardly fancy, but I was still a young and relatively inexperienced producer and all this felt like I was going up in the world.

I got the train to Newport and arrived there at about seven or eight at night. I was met by a guy called Kingsley Ward, who was there to drive me to the studio. He was a real character. Kingsley and his brother Charles had been in a band in the'60s. When that fizzled out, they had the idea of turning their old farm into a recording studio, despite it being miles from anywhere. It was a real *Field of Dreams* story. This most unlikely place went from a livestock farm full of pigs and cows to one of the most significant musical buildings in Britain. The number of massively important albums and songs that were made there is amazing – everything from Queen's 'Bohemian Rhapsody' to Oasis's 'Wonderwall' were recorded in those old barns. It's like a non-establishment Abbey Road.

Kingsley was very welcoming. As we were driving through all this dark countryside, leaving the lights of towns and cities behind, he told me that the band then using the studio had overrun. They were supposed to be finished, but they had needed to take an extra day. They'd be gone by tomorrow and my session wouldn't be affected, but it meant that their producer would still be in the producer's accommodation that night.

Kingsley told me not to worry about all this. As well as the main studio, they had an old barn over on the other side of the valley, which bands could use as a rehearsal space. A few years later, this would become Monnow Valley Studio, but back then it was still quite a rough, ramshackle old building called the Old Mill. 'We've got a band rehearsing in there now,' he told me, 'but there's only three of them and there's five beds. You wouldn't mind bunking in with them, would you? It'll only be for tonight.' I wasn't keen on spending the night in a room with a bunch of strangers, but I was out in the deepest countryside at night with no way to leave, so I pretty much had no choice but to do what they told me. I said, 'Do I have to sleep with a load of people that I don't know?' He said, 'Oh, you'll love them. A great bunch of lads, they're really nice.'

Kingsley drove up this dark, dark winding path to the old mill. He parked up and took me in. There was a band set up in the big room. Kingsley said, 'This is Ian, he's going to be staying in the spare bed tonight. So that's lovely. I'll leave you now. Ta-ra!', and he left and shut the door, and he was gone.

I turned around and these three black-clad wild-looking guys were staring at me, wondering who I was and what I was doing there. It was Lemmy, wearing his Nazi peaked cap and iron crosses, Fast Eddie and 'Filthy Animal' Taylor.

So that was how I met Motörhead, and that's why the four of us spent the night all snuggled up together, miles from anywhere in this old Welsh mill.

Over the years, I've recorded many times in Rockfield Studios. It's a unique and inspiring place to work and it has an uncanny habit of adapting in a subtle way to every band I've recorded there. All bands have their own unique experiences at Rockfield and they all seem to love it.

Sometime in the early '90s, I was travelling there with a band from Moston in Manchester who will have to remain nameless. They were not used to life outside of their city, and they were amazed by what they saw. On the drive in, we went through a small village which had two garages opposite each other, one selling Mercedes and the other BMWs. It caused quite a stir with the band. They were amazed that the cars on the forecourts had wheels and radios in them, and that they were left out for the night.

The next morning, at about 4 a.m., I was woken up by a strange sound. Looking out of my window onto the quadrangle, I saw two vans reversing. I thought nothing of it at the time and went back to sleep. At breakfast that day, I was sitting round the table with the band and their manager when the studio owner, Kingsley, opened the door. 'There's been quite a drama in the next village,' he said excitedly. 'All the cars on the forecourts have been stripped and left on bricks, with their wheels removed and the radios gone.'

All the heads around the table seemed to be staring intently into their cereal bowls in silence. I'm no Sherlock Holmes, but I suspect I could have solved the strange case of the Monmouth car strippers.

13

'HEY! LUCIANI'

In 1988, I produced the album *I Am Kurious Oranj* for the Fall. After we'd mixed it, I went to the Townhouse Studios to master it with a guy called Ian. It was all sounding great. Then, at some point, the lead singer Mark E. Smith arrived. He had a plastic carrier bag with him from Leo's, which was this supermarket in Manchester, with cans of beer in it.

Mark cracked open a beer, put his feet up and had a listen to what we'd done.

'That sounds alright,' he said. 'But when I was at home I got the cassette tape of the album you gave me and I played it on this.' He pulled out a crappy mono cassette player from his carrier bag. It was one of those machines that were used with early home computers for loading games – it had a tinny little speaker and wasn't really intended for playing music. He'd found it in the market just the week before and it was his latest toy. 'I thought it sounded a lot better on this than what you're doing here,' he said. 'So what we'll do is we'll put a mic on this tape player and play the tape and record how it sounds through this. Then we'll put that out instead.'

This was obviously a bad idea, but it was such a bad idea that it was quite hard to explain to him why we shouldn't do it. Mark loved a bit of mischief making and presenting you with a crazy conundrum. I think he just wanted to challenge you to see how you'd react. If you'd be brave enough to put up a fight, then you were okay. I was trying to come up with a calm, reasoned argument for why it wouldn't work, and why we weren't going to actually do that. As I was floundering about, Ian, the mastering engineer, left the room, went into the kitchen and came back with a bread knife. It was a huge thing, really massive. He showed it to Mark and looked him in the eye for a few seconds. Then he put it down on the mixing desk. He said, 'We'll just continue as we were, shall we?', and he calmly finished off mastering the album without looking up. When he left the room, Mark turned to me, laughed and said, 'He's great, that guy!'

To this day I still don't know if Mark genuinely wanted to record off the mono tape player, or if he just wanted to see how we'd react. I really liked Mark. He was a total eccentric and I thought he was hilarious. I know he could be the devil at times, but I just remember laughing loads when I was with him.

When I was young and first going to Eric's, before I was in a band, I'd often see the Fall playing. Everyone loved the Fall. We'd get to talk to them afterwards. Mark was already an odd character back then. Sometime later he asked me to record a single, which was 'Hey! Luciani'.

We recorded it in a studio on the outskirts of Liverpool, out past Fazakerley, in Kirkby. It was called Amazon Studios and it became my 'home' studio, really, the place I spent more time in than anywhere else. Later on, it would move to the centre of Liverpool and be renamed Parr Street Studios. At this point, however, it was in this brick hut in the middle of an MOT testing site just off the M57, next to a woodyard. It was owned by a guy whose father ran a company called Amazon Gas, which was based in this testing centre. There was a hut they didn't really use, so his son turned it into Amazon Studios.

There weren't a lot of decent studios in the northwest at the time, so it was pretty busy and you'd get all sorts using it. They had three studios there, plus one little lounge with a television in it that people in all the studios could use. You never knew who was going to be in the other studios, or who you'd meet in the lounge. It might be Dana, or it might be the Smiths, or it might be the cast from the BBC comedy *'Allo 'Allo!* The maddest collection of bands passed through there – there was James, the Spinners, the Waterboys, Ian Gillan, the Ruthless Rap Assassins and Dusty Springfield. Martin Hannett produced the Happy Mondays there and Ray Manzarek of the Doors produced the Bunnymen. I remember sitting in that lounge on a wreck of a sofa with Tony Iommi from Black Sabbath, watching the telly. I was trying to get up the courage to say, 'Do you mind if I turn over, Tony?' Julian Cope was in that lounge once, absolutely off his cake on something, when the police turned up. There were spliffs everywhere. As luck would have it, though, the police officer was a big fan and let him off.

Local Knotty Ash legend Ken Dodd came by once or twice. I always remember a time I'd come out of the studio and just happened to be standing in the reception area when Ken Dodd came up to me and tried to give me two hundred quid in cash. I said to him, 'I'm just standing here, I haven't done anything,' but he kept winking and telling me to take it. That was his thing – he used to pay everyone in cash. Later, he had all that problem with his tax and the Inland Revenue took him to court. They were confident that he would be sent down because they had found something like £300,000 in suitcases in his attic. But unfortunately for the

Revenue, this was a jury trial. Ken Dodd just told the jury a load of jokes in the courtroom. They loved him and found him not guilty, so he got off.

Amazon Studios was an amazing place in many ways, but outside it everything was pretty desolate. You were just out there in the wild and it was quite an intimidating place. It was near the estates at Simonswood, which at the time were rough as fuck. It was amazing that it didn't get robbed all the time. This was the place where I really learnt to be a producer, in among all that craziness.

When I arrived for the Fall session, I had never worked with Mark E. Smith before or even spoken to him properly on an equal level. I turned up on time and the band weren't there but Mark was waiting outside. His opening gambit was testing: 'I'm gonna go up to the pub for a bit,' he said. 'Maybe you could get on with the track? We haven't got a drummer at the moment, so you're going to have to programme the drums.' And I said, 'Hang on, I've not heard the song. Have you got a demo of it or something so I can hear it?' It turned out that he didn't. Instead, he turned to me and he said, 'It's like a snake, cock,' and he slapped me on the shoulder. Then he turned round and wandered off to find a pub.

The band turned up shortly after that and we got set up and got to work. All I had to be going on with as I programmed the drums was this comment, which was that the song was like a snake. And on the face of it, this was kind of nuts. But there was a real method in Mark's madness. It put such a responsibility and onus on you that the pressure would get you to try out things that you would normally never do. It was a brilliant way for an artist like him to bring out the best in everyone else. While he just went down the pub, I was trying to make the drums be like a snake and the band were playing around what I was doing. Somehow, we eventually got it together, just in time for Mark to get back.

I remember afterwards thinking that this was genius. We'd all just tried so hard and been so focused. Of course, I understand that this was equally an approach that could fall flat. Maybe many times when he did things like that, it did fall flat. Yet at times like this he managed to get people to produce things that they didn't know they were capable of. I think in a creative situation, if you can find a way of getting people to exceed their own expectations, then you're not stupid. Whether it was a conscious thing that Mark did, I don't know. It might have been that he was just an ornery character and letting others do things for him suited him very well, but, ultimately, if it worked then it worked. That's what matters.

With Mark, it was all about an idea. Sometimes putting limitations on things and narrowing the parameters to focus on an idea is a clever thing to do. If you have a good idea but don't do a good job getting the track recorded, then it's still a good idea and that will come through. If you don't have a good idea, then you can make the most brilliantly produced track, but it still won't be anything because it doesn't have anything at the heart of it. With 'Hey! Luciani', the idea was a song about the Pope, who died mysteriously after a month, with music that was like a snake. You can't really argue with that, can you?

After he got back from the pub, Mark didn't even comment on what we'd done. As he saw it, he was all about people doing their jobs. People were there to do what they were paid to do and they didn't need hand-holding or pats on the back. I remember him saying to me once, about a different song, 'I think you've completely got that track all wrong.' I asked him what was wrong with it and he said, 'Well, if I tell you that, I want your money.' His attitude was, you're the one we're paying so do your job and don't bother me.

It was around this time that I was starting to write my own songs. My fear was that if I didn't do this now, I was forever going to end up just being a producer of other people's stuff. I was chatting with Mark about all this and I had a couple of songs that I'd written. I ended up playing them to him. It makes me cringe now to think about it. I mean, this is not the sort of thing an artist expects to hear from the producer they've hired, who should be totally focused on their record and dedicated to the craft of producing. But Mark was amazingly supportive. He told me that I had to do it and he was just really encouraging. Ian McNabb of the Icicle Works was really positive as well. I don't think I would have had the confidence to actually record my own songs without his and Mark's encouragement.

The only problem was that he was insistent that I recorded under the name the Hordes of Broud. I told him that I was thinking of calling it the Lightning Seeds. He said no, it had to be the Hordes of Broud. He used to send me these lovely letters pushing me to do it and he'd include all these drawings that he'd done of these hordes with their bows and arrows and stuff. I wasn't convinced, but maybe there's another universe out there where 'Three Lions' was by Frank Skinner, David Baddiel and the Hordes of Broud.

The name the Lightning Seeds actually comes from me mishearing the lyrics to 'Raspberry Beret' by Prince. In that song, Prince sings about how the thunder drowns out what the lightning sees. When I heard it, I thought that he was singing about hanging out with the Lightning Seeds. I thought, 'Wow, who are the Lightning Seeds? I want to be hanging out with Prince and those guys! They sound like a cool bunch.'

Lightning itself is a symbol that musicians use a lot. Elvis had a lightning bolt on his 'taking care of business' logo, for example, and David Bowie had that iconic lightning bolt make-up on the cover of *Aladdin Sane*. Lighting symbolises the moment of inspiration, when a new idea arrives with a shock, as if out of nowhere, so you can see why musicians are drawn to it. Seeds are the opposite, in a way. An acorn contains a potential oak tree, but it needs time and nurturing. They represent the craft and effort needed to turn the moment of inspiration into a fully realised creative work. So there's a nice tension between the two words and one that sums up what creating music is about.

At one point in the late '90s, I went to get a haircut, but I was early for my appointment. I spoke to the barber and he told me to come back in fifteen minutes. When I returned, he told me that the guy in the chair earlier was Prince's manager and that he had asked the barber if I was the singer in the Lightning Seeds. The barber told him that I was and Prince's manager said, 'Tell him that Prince loves the story about mishearing his lyrics.' I couldn't believe it! It's quite something to realise that Prince knows you exist – I would never have had that moment if I'd have gone with the Hordes of Broud.

I've heard people talk about the dark side of Mark. As I see it, Mark E. Smith was always brilliantly Mark E. Smith – good or bad, he was definitely unique. I learnt stuff from him. I'm glad knew him and I really liked him. So thanks, Mark.

14

JOLLIFICATION

Around the time that the first stage of the Lightning Seeds came to a spluttering halt, in the early '90s, I read *The Adventures of Sherlock Holmes* by Sir Arthur Conan Doyle. In that book is a short story called 'The Adventure of the Blue Carbuncle'. Holmes was telling his colleague Doctor Watson about a man who, at 4 a.m. on Christmas morning, was returning home 'from some small jollification'. I thought to myself, 'Is "jollification" an *actual* word? How brilliant if it is.' I could imagine Holmes dismissing his cocaine binges as nothing more than a small jollification. It seemed to me that we could all do with a little jollification of our own every now and again. I had not done any work on another Lightning Seeds album at that point, but

I immediately knew I had the title. When you name something that doesn't exist and which you have no ideas for, it suddenly sparks into life: it has potential. I began to think about the album that would become *Jollification*.

I'd always had it in my head that the Lightning Seeds project would last for three albums. The problem was that after I'd done the first two, it had kind of ground to a halt. I had no record label, and no manager, and of course no band. I had never even played a gig as the Lightning Seeds. No one was calling me up or asking anything of me. The Lightning Seeds only existed if I decided that it existed when I got out of bed that morning. If I didn't think about it, it didn't exist. And it became quite easy to not think about it.

It was quite a nice time in my life, really. In 1991, Riley had been born, so being a new dad took up a good slice of my attention. I was living in a house opposite Strawberry Field, so I could see the famous gates on the opposite side of the road from my window. Plus I was producing again and enjoying it this time. I worked on albums by people like Alison Moyet and Terry Hall, and bands like Dodgy and the Frank and Walters. I was working with Cenzo Townshend, a brilliant engineer and a lovely guy. He was a genius in the architecture of sound and I would have been lost without him. We made a great team. Cenzo who I mentioned earlier was an important player on 'Pure', was quite posh, but he moved up to Chester from the south so that he could work with me. He engineered everything I did for about eight years and we just worked well together. He's since gone on to become incredibly successful, mixing some really great records.

I had, for the first time in my life, a studio of my own. It was in a place called 'The Laboratory'. This was an old building with thick stone walls. Carved into the stone above the doors was a date in the 1800s and the words 'The Laboratory', so I can only assume it must have been an actual laboratory in the nineteenth century. I rented a room in there that was downstairs and to the right. It wasn't far from the centre of Liverpool, but it was still quite a rough area. There was a big block of derelict flats which was maybe four or five storeys high opposite, with all the windows put through. No one lived there, but there were a lot of junkies and homeless people around. It was a bit of a no-man's land, really, all a bit overlooked and unadopted. There were no markings on the road and things like that, so people would just use it as someplace to park when they were going into town. It could be quite intimidating. But – it was a studio of my own, at last.

It would have been very easy to forget all about the Lightning Seeds at that point. I wasn't sitting there thinking about how that part of my life had ended or how I could get back on track. I don't think I even noticed that no one had called or mentioned it for ages. It felt to me like it had been a successful venture. I was quite wrong about this as it really hadn't been that successful at all. But I had stood up and presented myself as a songwriter and a singer and I'd come up with songs like 'Pure' and 'The Life of Riley' and that made quite a difference to me on a personal level. Maybe that was why I felt comfortable producing all of a sudden, because I had scratched that itch and done the thing that I was frightened to do.

The A&R man who was working with Dodgy was a guy called David Rose. He was from A&M Records and it turned out that he wanted to sign me to make another Lightning Seeds album. This news came as quite a surprise. I'd usually been the underdog on these fly-by-night little indie labels at a time when a lot of Liverpool bands were getting great and lucrative record contracts from major labels. I thought, 'Oh, a proper label wants me, that's quite exciting.'

So I had an album title, a studio and a reason to work on some new songs. That was enough for the Lightning Seeds to spark back into life – by which I mean I would wake up in the morning and be thinking of them. The way I tend to work is to roughly record any melodies or song ideas that I have. When I've got them on tape, I quickly move on and forget all about them and see what else I can come up with. These days, I just do this by humming into my phone. I leave them for months and then see if they're any good when I come back. It's like a test for them – if they still sound good when I go back to them, then I should probably work on them further. Back then in The Laboratory, I had a portable studio set-up. Ian Skinnie, my assistant engineer, would get me a cup of tea, I'd have my acoustic guitar and I'd be away. The plan was that I would put down the ideas I had and once I'd worked out four or five songs, then I'd start recording them properly.

When I got to the point where I had my four or five songs, however, someone put a window through and broke into my studio at night. They stole a lot of things, one of which was my guitar, which was really upsetting. I loved that guitar. I'd had it since I was a kid. My brother Robert had been to America and brought it back as a present for me. I never saw it again and was just devastated to lose it. The other significant things that were nicked were the portable studio and a little cassette machine. Between them, they contained the only record of the *Jollification* songs.

There was nothing else for it but to reset and start again. I had the window fixed and got a new portastudio and some replacement equipment, but I had no record of the songs or any real memory of how they went. Those original *Jollification* songs were gone for good. I tried my best to put them down on tape again as well as I could remember, but I know that I didn't get them right. They were a vague approximation of what I thought they were, but they weren't really the same. It was those half-remembered and very different versions of the songs that became what everyone now knows as the album *Jollification*. The real *Jollification* is lost. It's become a bit mythic to me because those songs were far from finished but they were brimming with potential. Sometimes I dream of listening to the album that they would have become. I expect that the thief probably just binned the tapes so they could sell on the gear, but sometimes I wonder if they kept them or had a listen. If they did, they are the only person who knows what the real *Jollification* sounds like. I have no clue.

At the time I was producing an album for Alison Moyet. Working in the studio with a singer as good as that is one of the more enjoyable things a producer can do. Her A&R person was a guy from Buckinghamshire called Rob Stringer and he came up to hear what we were doing. After Alison left, he stayed around chatting. He said, 'You know, I was a big fan of the Lightning Seeds. Do you not do that any more?' So I explained that I was working on a few songs which had been stolen, but I was coming up with some half-remembered versions of them. He said, 'Can I hear them?' I had bits of programmed drums on tape at that point, so I played the tapes and sang along and played guitar while I was sat on the couch to give him as good a sense of them as I could. He said, 'I love these. I really want to sign you to Sony.' He got his boss up from London to Liverpool for a night, a guy called Paul, and I played him the songs as well – I think it was 'Lucky You', 'Marvellous' and a couple of others. I didn't have all the words and they were far from finished, but it was enough.

I was wondering what to do about both Sony and A&M being interested in me when I got a call from Dick Leahy – the guy who had put out 'Pure'. He said, 'Ian, I'm sitting here with Rob Kahane, who manages George Michael. He's got a label deal through Hollywood Records in LA. He really wants to sign the Lightning Seeds to do an album.'

Rob Kahane was this big American manager and I'd always done better in America than Britain, so I knew I should think about this seriously. During my MCA days, I had had a string of songs that had been big in the college charts. I used to get recognised walking around New York because my videos were played on MTV a lot. Then I would come back home to the UK and be anonymous again. That worked well for me, that situation – I must admit I quite liked that. Even I could see that signing with a big label in America was exactly what I should have been trying to do.

I also found that I really liked Rob Stringer. This was unusual because, in Liverpool at the time, the idea that you'd actually like a record company guy was a bit heretical. It was usually much more adversarial. The big labels were seen as the enemy. There was a sense that, if you could get them to sign you and give you some money, the thing to do was to spend it all on drugs as quickly as you could, before they could ask for it back, or to cut them out of the creative process and spend years arguing. That sort of self-sabotage was a very common pitfall for Liverpool bands at the time, and many amazing bands and records were lost to it. That was a path I didn't wish to follow. I decided to resist the peer pressure of heroic failure.

The more I spoke with Rob Stringer, however, the more I found that I liked him. After years of dealing with indie labels, it felt strange to find someone I felt I could trust at the largest of all the majors. As we worked together, it became obvious how lucky that chance meeting in the studio was. For the first time, I had someone at the record company I felt was genuinely on my side. He had levels of belief and energy that I had never encountered before.

His career has been meteoric. He went from strength to strength after this and he's now the chairman of Sony Music Group and CEO of Sony Music Entertainment. This makes perfect sense to me because, even back then, I could tell that he was brilliant at what he does. He changed the course of my career and my life, and he's still a great friend to this day. Even his great love of Luton Town FC has made them become like a second team to me.

I signed with Sony, but it left me with the hard task of refusing the A&M Records offer at the last minute. I thought that it would be wrong to tell them over the phone, so I got on the train to London. I've always tried to be honest even when it is a hard conversation, because I find that although people might get angry, it doesn't tend to last or to linger in quite the same way as when you aren't brave enough to tell them the truth. It's crazy now to think of how worried I was back then about having to deal with all these different offers without upsetting anyone.

Telling the unfiltered truth, of course, can have its drawbacks. Ideally, I'd employ a level of tact whenever I'm being honest, but I don't always remember to do this. Sometimes when I have been too preoccupied with music or focused on other matters, I have blurted out things that I shouldn't. For example, Dick Leahy once invited me to lunch with George Michael and I was asked if I would be interested in potentially working with George. My immediate reply was, 'I just don't think I want to work with someone who is stoned all the time.' I didn't think anything of this after I said it and we carried on with our dinner, but George must have thought, 'What a twat!' He wouldn't have been wrong. I lack a filter sometimes, and always regret it later when I realise what I've done.

The reason I said that, of course, was because it was true: I was explaining what I felt. Now, though, I cringe at the thought of it and wish I had said something tactful. I know I reacted like that because I had just been in the studio with a certain Liverpool band who'll remain nameless and they were useless stoned bastards throughout. It had been incredibly hard work and incredibly frustrating, so my reaction to George was just me being truthful. I do wish, however, that I'd sugar-coated my response a bit. George, to his credit, took it very well, and then nipped out for a spliff.

I think I'm better now, but when I was younger I could be really socially oblivious. I think this must be the reason I offended Jarvis Cocker. I was once asked to do a mix on a Pulp track. This was in the early '90s, before they had had their hits, and for some reason Jarvis was in Lark Lane in Liverpool, so he said perhaps I could bring the mix over when it was done. I drove over and got out of the car as he came out and I handed the tape to him. This was the only time we've ever met. He asked if it sounded good and I said, 'I dunno. I don't think I've nailed it. It was difficult and it wasn't recorded in a way that I could do what I wanted to do to it.' My head was still in the studio, really. I tried to explain how I thought it should be done. In my head, the track was still in bits and I was still thinking about how it should all fit together. Somehow, in this fairly brief conversation, I must have really offended him, although, unfortunately, I failed to notice this. He was very cold and wouldn't come near me after that. I guess a wiser person would have been tactful, but *c'est la vie*.

Rob's offer to sign me came with a condition: I had to fully commit to it and stop everything else that I was doing. I had to live it. I had to be an artist. I had to form a band and play gigs, and I had to stop producing. He was absolutely right about this, but I needed someone to tell me. Nowadays I think it's fairly normal to be both a producer and an artist, especially in hip hop, but it was very unusual back then. I did need to focus all my energies on this next album and give it my all.

So I stopped being a producer. I had started working on a second Dodgy album, but I stepped away after only doing a few tracks. I introduced them to a producer called Hugh Jones, who I thought would be great for them. Luckily, the band and their A&R man, David, who I'd just pissed off by not signing with him, agreed that Hugh would work. He finished off that record, which was to become *Homegrown* (1994), and continued working with them on the next, so that all worked out okay.

As I was finishing off my final production assignment, the Alison Moyet record, at Townhouse Studios in London, Damon Albarn and Graham Coxon from Blur came to see me. They'd just done *Modern Life Is Rubbish* (1993). They said that they really liked my stuff and asked me to produce their next album, which would have been *Parklife* (1994). I think they were big fans of Terry Hall and were impressed that I'd done songs like 'Sense' with him. I liked them a lot and I really would have loved to have worked on *Parklife*, so the offer was a bit of a test for me. Ultimately, I turned it down because of my promise to Rob that I would commit to the Lightning Seeds. I can't say I regret doing that, because it turned out well for everyone. Stephen Street went on to produce that album and that worked out brilliantly, and I focused on *Jollification*. I made the right decision, but I bet I would have really enjoyed making *Parklife*.

With the business and career side of things in hand, I had no excuse. I had to make the record and it had to live up to all the faith that people were showing in me. I went into the studio with Cenzo Townshend by my side, as well as Simon Rogers, who I had met when I was producing the Fall years before and who had helped me when I was making *Sense* in my brother's spare room. Simon was really good at programming and loops and stuff like that. We ended up working together a lot over the years. I would almost say that during that recording, me, Cenzo and Simon were like a band in a way, even though Cenzo was an engineer rather than a musician. We were a team. It was just three guys making a record. We all just got on with it. It felt like a band because it wasn't just me in charge, telling them what to do. We'd all argue, we all cared about it. I'd suggest something and if it was a shit idea, they'd just say no.

Because I still didn't have a band and didn't have a drummer, we worked in a similar way to *Sense*, in that we built the songs out of loops. There are no real drums on *Jollification* at all, it's all loops or programming. If you listen to a track like 'Lucky You', you'll see that there are hardly any drums on that. There's a sampled bass drum sound, along with me hitting a massive tambourine and also some clapping, but there are no drums in the normal sense. No one ever notices. Later on, this would make it tricky to work out how to do the song live, but it shows what you can get away with when you have to. We did it in such a way that you wouldn't notice because the focus was on the song.

We had an S900 sampler, but there were no computers in those days to control everything, so it was really difficult to get the loops to work. It took a lot of messing about. A lot of the songs on *Jollification* are in the wrong key for me because it was so hard to get the loops working properly. To make it work, we had to let them control the key and the tempo. A few years after this, the technology advanced and it became much easier to work in that way. It has become pretty much the norm. At the time though, it felt exciting because it was like heading off into unexplored territory.

Jollification was probably the most collaborative album that I'd done. I'd always thought of different bands as being like all these little planets in their own orbit, with their own distinct perspectives and different ways of thinking and working. Because I'd always been a bit on the outside, I hadn't settled on one of these planets, but I had visited a number of them and knew how different they were. I thought that an album could be a great excuse to collaborate with all these people who maybe would never leave their own worlds or cross over those borders. I think I wanted to put things together that might not otherwise meet and *Jollification* enabled me to do that a little more. I ended up writing a song with Terry Hall, a song with Alison Moyet and a song with Ian McNabb. They all sang on the album and so did a few others, like Simon Fowler from Ocean Colour Scene. I knew this great organ player called Clive Layton, he used to bring his Hammond organ over from Coventry. Dave Bascombe is a really great mix engineer, one who has been crucial to a lot of the Lightning Seeds' records, and the album really came together when he got to work on it. And of course, there was Simon doing the programming and Cenzo engineering. It was a really enjoyable way of working.

Jollification wasn't an immediate hit. The first thing we did was release 'Lucky You' as a single, but it pretty much vanished without a trace. This was where Rob Stringer at Sony really proved himself. Other record companies might have cut their losses and started to concentrate their efforts elsewhere at that point, but Rob still believed in me and in *Jollification*. He had boundless energy; he went round every person in the building, hassling them into giving their everything. He kept the company focused on fully supporting the record. Without Rob, this chapter of the Lightning Seeds wouldn't have happened. He was pure energy, like a gale blowing behind you, which filled the sails of your ship and kept you on course. What's great about him is that he'll give you good news and he'll give you bad news – most people in the industry won't give you bad news.

When the album was released in 1994, it wasn't an immediate hit, but it just hung around and it kept selling. It stayed round the charts for well over a year. And despite never getting into the top ten, it ultimately sold over a million copies in the UK. During this time, Sony kept pushing singles. 'Change' was the second single. That managed to break the charts and went top twenty. Then came

'Marvellous' and 'Perfect', followed by a re-release of 'Lucky You'. None of the singles went that high in the charts, but they were always on the radio and they stayed in the charts for long periods. You couldn't really avoid them.

The aspects of those songs which were positive and uplifting, and which had been quite a radical shock to the northern indie scene I came out of, suddenly seemed to fit the times. People understood what it was that I was trying to do in a way that they didn't with my earlier albums. They were ready and eager for the energy of Britpop and, at that point in the mid-'90s, my record made total sense. Timing is so important for bands.

When I recorded my album, I knew exactly what the Lightning Seeds were about and how they should sound. Like I said, I had the title *Jollification* from the start and that summed up what I was trying to do well because the remit for the Lightning Seeds was to be uplifting. There needed to be positivity among the difficult emotions. It sounds simple, but it's quite hard to do something up and positive that isn't banal and vacuous. You need to have different layers in there, both lyrically and musically. There needs to be honesty and openness and nuance. It's a finely balanced thing and it's very easy to get it wrong. Sad songs are much easier to write – it's quite a straightforward emotion that you are aiming for.

Because of my background, many people were surprised by how uplifting the Lightning Seeds were. They assumed that I would have made music with that bleak, epic, northern sound, like the Bunnymen or Joy Division. I didn't feel any need to repeat what those bands did, though, because they'd already done it and they did it brilliantly.

Thinking back now, it's noticeable that *Jollification* was recorded in this quite bleak environment, with the thieves and the drug addicts and the condemned tower blocks all around. There are a lot of records that pretend that they come from a place like that. When you genuinely are in a dark place, though, you're not going to glorify or celebrate it. To wallow in bleakness is a form of indulgence that not everyone can afford. Instead, you have to create light. That's the most human response to the world we're in: you create light and you use that light to illuminate your world and transform it into something bearable.

I always liked uplifting psychedelic pop. When I talk about pop here, I'm using that word in terms of people like Andy Warhol or Roy Lichtenstein. It's that bright, clear moment, like you get in Pop Art. That's what I was trying to do with the Lightning Seeds. My aspiration, as I've said, was always to create something like 'See Emily Play' by Pink Floyd. It had psychedelia, charm, a chorus and it is otherworldly. It's magic. For me, that's a perfect pop record. So

I wanted to make music like that because I loved it, but at the same time it was just the right thing to do.

When the album was recorded, the label started talking about the cover art and they came up with various suggestions. I remember they were keen to go with an image of some chattering teeth. I thought, 'No, that's not what this is at all.' It should be something simple, positive, good and grasped in an instant. I was thinking in terms of Warhol's soup can, something fairly everyday but which just jumps out. Like a strawberry. A strawberry felt like it could be a great Pop Art image. It's bright red, like a certain football team I could mention. The taste of a strawberry is an immediate vivid experience, lovely and sweet and unlike anything else. A strawberry just is what it is – you can't debate strawberries and you can't dismiss them. You see a strawberry and you get exactly what it is. That's what I wanted the Lightning Seeds to be.

The final cover with the big bright strawberry in the sky was created by the designer Mark Farrow, who has done loads of iconic sleeves for people like the Pet Shop Boys, Spiritualized and the Manic Street Preachers. It was a piece of design genius, something that lived long in people's memories. I was delighted with it. It really captured what the album was. The original versions of the album and CD had scratch-and-sniff covers – you scratched the sleeve and you could smell strawberries. I did wonder if anyone would ever accuse us of ripping off the sleeve from *The Velvet Underground & Nico* album, which was just a Pop Art image of a banana. That album cover was definitely an influence.

If you think of this rundown and dingy corner of Liverpool and then imagine a giant strawberry emerging from a building, huge and fresh and bright – that's pretty much how I remember the making of *Jollification*.

15

'I WAS LOOKING IN
THE WRONG DRAWER'

After the *Jollification* album was released in 1994, it was time to confront my fear of being a frontman and singing live. I had to live up to my promise and go out on the road with a full band as the Lightning Seeds.

To test the waters, we booked a gig in a pub somewhere in Yorkshire. I had no idea if anyone would come. Then the guy at the venue phoned up. He told me that it was selling great and that there were hardly any tickets left. I was made up by this. I started to entertain the idea that maybe I would find a live audience after all. A couple of days before the gig, he phoned back and said, 'Sorry, I was looking in the wrong drawer. I've had a "sold out" notice up for ages, but all the tickets are in the other drawer.' It was not the most auspicious start to my live career. I was already incredibly nervous about performing in front of an audience as it was and this did not help my confidence.

Once I had finally decided I was going to play live shows, I had to decide what kind of band I wanted the Lightning Seeds to be.

It also meant recruiting the right musicians. On Lightning Seeds records, I always tried to find musicians who had played in bands rather than regular session musicians. I can't stress how different those two options are, or how much they affect the resulting music. I firmly believe that there are people who played great and people who played great things, and I very much wanted the latter – people who are creative and channelled their charm and love into the playing, not ruthlessly efficient technicians.

The other big decision I made was that I wouldn't recreate the records – I would play the songs. This would allow the musicians space for creativity and wouldn't date the band in the way a recording might. The band could then be a developing entity. This has turned out to be a great idea.

I hoped that the Lightning Seeds might become a group as well as a solitary venture, but the world of live music felt alien to me, and I had a lot to learn. It took me a very long time to become comfortable on stage singing, enjoying myself and getting lost in the moment. There have been some great moments and brilliant people have passed through and worked with the Lightning Seeds. The line-up has changed a lot over the years. The one constant has been Martyn Campbell on bass, who has always had that creativity in his approach and channels emotion into every note. His obsession for music matches my own.

At the heart of the group there's my son Riley on guitar. I love having Riley on stage. There's a big tradition of brothers or siblings in bands, from the Beach Boys to Oasis, and it's commonly accepted that their closeness does bring something to the party. There's a lot fewer fathers and sons in bands, but I do think a similar thing happens. Family is a connection, and musicians need a connection. It might seem like a bit of a mad set-up, especially when he's there playing 'The Life of Riley', which is about him being born, but it works. Plus he's a great guitarist and I get to be proud of him for that. One of his first ever gigs was when we played the Pyramid Stage at Glastonbury in 2010, when he was about twenty. There are not many people who could handle something like that at that age, but he did. Afterwards, I said, 'Did you see the size of that crowd!', and he said, 'No.' He had focused so completely on what he was playing that he didn't look at the sea of faces.

I am aware that a band is always changing, but at the moment I adore playing with the people I share the stage with, like the drummer Jim Sharrock, who has known and grown up with Lightning Seeds' music since he was a little kid, because his uncle Chris was our drummer for the time around *Jollification* and *Dizzy Heights*. He and Riley have both become superb musicians, unfazed by any challenge. Finally, Adele Emmas on keyboards is a singer and songwriter herself, and she's been the essential final piece of the jigsaw.

I think one of the reasons I loved being in the studio is that, although I was sometimes socially awkward, it gave me a feeling of community. I was able to really connect with people in a way that I found difficult to achieve outside of that environment. That ritual of routine in recording has largely disappeared now, and a lot of time is spent on the computer, often with no one else around. Perhaps that's why I now enjoy playing live so much. In the same way the studio used to be, this is now my chance to hang out with musicians, and of course the crew and the audiences as we play and travel wherever the music takes us. I've really ended up as a troubadour.

In the early days of the Lightning Seeds, I loved being in the studio around the brilliant bands I was working with. Simon Rogers was a massive inspiration. He was a string arranger, brilliant guitarist and a master of the sampler and keyboards. Simon, Cenzo Townshend, Dave Bascombe and I spent so much time together in all sorts of homemade studios. I remember those days as full of creativity, jokes and camaraderie. In many ways, these were my halcyon days and the happiest times of my life, recording until all hours of the night before returning home to a young Riley and probably my soulmate, his beautiful mother, Becky.

In the studio, you are in control and everything makes sense – at least in theory. Going out and playing live, by contrast, drops you into a world that is crazy and un-predictable, and quite often just ridiculous. One of the first gigs we played in Italy was in a café in Naples. The venue put on gigs with bands and could hold an audience of about 250 people, but at the same time, it was just a café. While we were soundchecking in the afternoon, the power went off for a couple of minutes. Afterwards I asked what had happened. They said that when they put the machine on to make a cheese toastie, it tended to over-load the power if someone was on stage at the same time. 'Obviously, you won't be selling any cheese toasties tonight when we're playing?' I nervously asked. They said, 'No, if someone orders one, then we have to make it.'

That evening, just after we got on stage and started play-ing 'Sense' there was a bang and all the power went off. We all looked at each other, then I looked over at the bar and sure enough, there they were, making a cheese toastie.

Our drummer Chris wasn't at all fazed. He kept playing the intro to 'Sense' and then he turned it into a drum solo to fill the time. He was jamming away until the toaster popped up and the guy flipped the switch. Then the power came back on stage and we played the rest of 'Sense' like nothing had happened. But, for the rest of the gig, I was dreading that happening again. You know what cheese toasties are like! If you see someone having one, then you want one as well. Being in a band is often described in glamorous terms, but no one warns you that sometimes you come lower down the pecking order than the hot bar snacks.

Touring can be hard, especially given the lack of sleep when travelling overnight on a tour bus. It can wear you down and sometimes you really suffer. Once we flew to Tokyo to do four shows in two days and I got on the plane not realising that I had an abscess in my mouth, underneath a crown. By the time I got off the plane, I was in agony. I was up all night hitting the walls; I didn't speak Japanese and couldn't even get a painkiller. Somehow, I managed to make it through the first couple of shows before the woman who was looking after us there got me an appointment with an American dentist. He said, 'If I sort this out now, you won't be able to sing tonight but I can give you some serious painkillers to get you through and then you can get it sorted when you get home.' I don't know what he gave me, but they put me in a really strange place. I was never quite all there after that, and it was an odd way to experience Japan, but I got through the rest of the shows with those painkillers and brandy.

There was never any question, even with all that pain, of abandoning the gigs. The only time I've cancelled a tour was when I ended up in hospital in Munich. I got a kidney stone because I became so dehydrated travelling around Europe on the tour bus. It made me really ill and they thought my appendix had burst. Generally, though, unless you've been hospitalised, you keep doing the gigs.

I was talking to Will Sergeant from the Bunnymen recently and saying how lucky we were to still be grabbing our guitars and going out on stage, even though we're both in our mid-sixties. Of all the people who started out with us, most of them have peeled off along the way. They've gone and become teachers or something sensible, but for some reason me and Will are lifers. He said, 'No, it's not luck. We both know that you can never quit.' This comes back to what I was talking about earlier – how you need a bit of steel to make it in the music business. The artist side of you needs to be sensitive and open, but you won't get anywhere unless you have that strength also.

After *Jollification* came out, we finally played a few gigs in America, but it was all pretty shambolic and the gigs were hardly advertised. We started by playing a string of bars down the Pacific Coast Highway. It was fun in a way, but it was hardly going to put us on the map. I remember playing a strange and very modern-looking venue in Texas. After the gig, the dressing room emptied out and it was just me in there when this troubled-looking Texan guy walked in. In his fifties, he was dressed a bit cowboy-ish. He looked really out of place for that type of gig. He introduced himself and said, 'I came to the gig because my son was a massive fan of your song "Pure". He bought it after he had split up with his girlfriend, who was the love of his life. He used to play the song in his room over and over and over again. Not long afterwards, he killed himself.'

As he was saying this, he was looking at me in a really weird way as if he was trying to decide what to do. He was a broken man. This being America, I had an irrational but very real worry that he might take out a gun and shoot me. I felt genuinely scared. I didn't know if he was blaming me for what happened to his son, but I was conscious that he had waited until I was alone in the dressing room before he came in. It was as if he needed someone to blame for his suffering. If he could bump me off, someone adjacent to the tragedy albeit obliquely, then maybe the pain would stop.

In an act of self-preservation, I gave him a hug. It threw him. 'I know how hard that can be,' I sympathised. 'I really feel for you. I've got a son too. I don't know what I would do if something like that happened to him. I hope that my song at least made your son feel better for a while.' The guy just looked at me. He nodded and said, 'Thank you,' and then left.

This incident really brought home to me the effect that music can have and the often bizarre connections that it creates between people. You have a thought and an idea and gradually, it turns into a song. You then record it – and at that time I would have recorded it in my house, or in my brother's house. It then gets turned into a record and that record is somehow beamed magically across the whole planet. I don't understand the science of how that happens, I just know that you turn your thoughts and emotions into melody, which is then sprinkled over the world. Some people who it is sprinkled on relate to it in a profound way. They may be someone who is very different to you and who you know nothing about, but a connection has still been made. It's as if there is a string from your head, going through the air and connecting in some weird fucking way to their head. And sometimes I feel those connections. It's not tangible, but I feel them.

Sometimes it's easy to dismiss thoughts like that but then you travel 5,000 miles across the world and you stand up in front of a room full of strangers. You sing a melody you wrote to describe an emotion you had back in Liverpool and all those people get it. They understand. Going out on the road and playing gigs teaches you that music is such an international language. At times like that, you know that the connection between you all is very magical and very real.

16

'WHO DO YOU THINK YOU ARE'

In March 1997, I presented the BBC music programme *Top of the Pops*. One of the strangest things about this experience was that I was comfortable enough with the idea to be able to do it. There I was, with a big golden microphone and my best blue top on, looking down the camera while I counted down the charts and introduced viewers to the likes of Sash!, Kula Shaker and Ant & Dec. I still had my dark sunglasses to hide behind, of course, but overall, I managed to take it all in my stride. I even got to introduce Dodgy as my 'showbiz pals', like an old-school Radio 1 DJ.

That's not to say that I was great at it, of course. It took a few takes to get my lines right. This was especially annoying for the Spice Girls. They were number one with

'Who Do You Think You Are', which was also the official Comic Relief charity single. I was stood in the crowd in front of the stage and the idea was that I was going to do my link to camera and introduce them while the song started playing and they were performing their dance routine in the background. If we timed it right, they would then start singing just as I finished my spiel. I kept messing up my lines, however, which meant that they kept having to reset for another take and restart their routine. They had to start off in these mad *Charlie's Angels*-type poses each time we reset. This didn't look that comfortable, not least because some of them had some really massive shoes on, which made everything a challenge. So they were none too happy about me messing up all the time, but still – we got it done.

The fact that I was presenting *Top of the Pops* is an indication of how, after *Jollification*, I had quickly become accepted by the Britpop-era music world. With my singles constantly on the radio, I found myself tolerated by the industry in a way I'd never experienced before. I was in my late thirties at the time. In theory, I was much older than I should have been to make it as a popstar, but the stars of Britpop did tend to be older than the stars of earlier music scenes. Britpop was not something that mainly came from teenagers, like punk had been. Bands who were genuinely a bunch of kids, like Supergrass or Ash, were the exception rather than the rule. People like Jarvis Cocker and Noel Gallagher were also in their thirties and like me, they had been plugging away at music for years, waiting for their chance. I was probably the oldest of the lot, but in this context I didn't seem too out of place. Needless to say, we were all pretty much in denial about this.

If ever I'm asked to define what a Britpop band was, I say that it was pretty much anyone who had a single out in the UK between about 1993 and 1997. That was enough to make you Britpop because otherwise there was no other connection that I could see. Blur and Oasis, for example, have little in common musically. The Lightning Seeds were different again, but we released records during this period, so we are classed as Britpop. But, although musically it was all over the shop, there was a shared attitude around that, in some ways, reminded me of Eric's in the post-punk era. There were all these big personalities around who were desperate to be noticed. There were a lot of ambitious, driven people mingling with and trying to outdo each other. There were people who were deeply into music, others who were in it for attention and fame. We all knew that where we were was the most interesting place to be at that point in time. What I learnt from Eric's was that, while I was in no way a rock star with a massive ego and bags of confidence, I was able to move in those circles and be accepted, provided that people were impressed by my music. If you can't command the stage like Mick Jagger, then you can still go to the party – you just need to have better songs.

One odd thing about Britpop was that earlier music scenes tended to be focused on a club, or perhaps a radio show or a magazine. There might have been fanzines and tape-trading communities as well. Somewhere there would be a community of like-minded kids creating something new, and occasionally – just occasionally – all that activity might briefly make it onto TV. With Britpop, however, television was pretty integral to it from the start. It was when you were backstage at a lot of those shows that you would get to meet other bands and hang out.

Of all the shows, it was Chris Evans' *TFI Friday* on Channel 4 that was closest to my heart. Chris was a great supporter of the band. We played that show often and it was always chaotic and always exciting. Chris was an exceptional broadcaster and he always seemed to be operating on a level way above all the other producers and presenters. He also seemed to embody the spirit of those times, for good or ill.

TFI Friday came back for a one-off twentieth anniversary special in 2015 and if anything, this was even more chaotic than it was back in the day. I was drafted into a band with Liam Gallagher, Roger Daltrey, Bonehead and Zak Starkey.

It was billed as a blokey supergroup, even if I was considerably less super than some of the others. We decided to do a cover of the Who's 'My Generation'. Along with '(I Can't Get No) Satisfaction', this was one of those great '60s anthems of frustrated male energy. Roger Daltrey was in his seventies at this point, but there he was with his great voice, singing about how he hoped he would die before he got old. The *TFI Friday* special was a '90s nostalgia exercise, but what we did was to pile nostalgia upon nostalgia. The show used to be filmed at Riverside Studios at Hammersmith. This had just closed and been knocked down, which helped make the original shows in the '90s feel like a long-gone golden age. We were then pushing all this '60s nostalgia on top of that. Instead of just revisiting the '90s, it felt like we were staking our claim to be part of a long, ongoing tradition.

When I signed to Sony, I had a meeting with a really lovely woman called Deirdre, who was in charge of getting acts on the TV. She said to me, 'We're trying to get you on the cooler shows. Don't worry, I won't put you forward for the kids' shows.' I told her that I would love to do the kids' shows. This surprised her, but when I was growing up, those shows meant the world to me. There was a programme in the north of England called *Lift Off with Ayshea* and another called *Do Not Adjust Your Set*, a forerunner to Monty Python.

I used to race home from school to catch the *Lulu* show, which was on at five o'clock. All these were kid shows, but it was through them that I discovered Jimi Hendrix, Cream, Marc Bolan, David Bowie and bands like that. They were all playing live and they were amazing. When people talk about the history of rock, they usually talk about people tuning in to Radio Caroline or *The Old Grey Whistle Test* and discovering all those bands that way, but I first saw Jimi Hendrix on the *Lulu* show. A lot of those performances have been lost now. The tapes of all the episodes of *Lift Off with Ayshea* were scheduled to be digitised, but there was a mix-up and they were all wiped instead.

I wanted to be on kids' programmes because I found my own music through those shows. Deirdre started booking us on programmes like *Live & Kicking*. We'd be up early on Saturday mornings to mime for Zoë Ball and Andi Peters, while Trevor & Simon mucked about, dancing in front of us. I mean, what's not to love about that? Even better, I could take Riley along because he was just the right age for things like *Live & Kicking* and loved going to studios. He also loved Zig & Zag, who were these two Irish alien puppets who appeared on the *Big Breakfast*. We'd go and mime to our single on *The Big Breakfast* and Zig & Zag would play in the band instead of our regular drummer and keyboard player. I'd been on *The Big Breakfast* so often that eventually they said, 'We're always interviewing you, could Zig & Zag interview Riley instead?' So that became my son's TV debut, at the age of about seven. He didn't have any front teeth then and was incredibly cute. He was a total professional and managed not to look down at the people operating the puppets, even though he really wanted to. They asked him what he thought of his dad's music. He said that he quite liked it, but what he liked the best was the Manic Street Preachers.

I think because it was known that we were willing to do those programmes, we kept getting offered more and more. We'd play on things like *This Morning* or the *Noel's House Party* New Year special, where we played 'Sugar Coated Iceberg' in front of one of the most hyped-up audiences I'd ever seen. A lot of bands were too cool to do things like that. On some levels this probably worked against us. It may have played into the perception that we weren't right for the more serious music shows, but I don't regret it for a minute – those kids' shows were much more fun.

17

'THREE LIONS'

Sometime after *Jollification* came out, around the time that I started working on my next album, *Dizzy Heights*, I got a message out of the blue from the Football Association. They asked if I would be interested in doing the official song for the England team for Euro 96. I still don't know why they asked me but I strongly suspect that it may well be because *Match of the Day* used an instrumental version of 'Life of Riley' for the Goal of the Month round-up. They must have thought, 'That music works well for football, we'll have some more of that.'

Oddly enough, when I had been in Big in Japan in the post-punk days, I co-wrote an instrumental with Bill Drummond that needed a title. I thought that it sounded like it would make a good theme tune for *Match of the Day,* so that's what I called it – 'Match of the Day'. Then in 1979, the Open Eye Gallery put out a compilation album called *Street to Street: A Liverpool Album,* featuring songs from new and unsigned local bands. We recorded 'Match of the Day' as our contribution. That album is best remembered now for containing the first released Echo & the Bunnymen track, a song called 'Monkies'. That was the closing track, while 'Match of the Day' opened the album. The late John Peel wrote the sleeve notes. He described our track as a 'little gem, which reasserts the strength of the twangy guitar in a perverse little theme that would have made John Barry spit with impotent rage fifteen years ago.' That's still probably my best write-up.

That track was the first song of mine to be released and, given what has happened since, the fact that it was called 'Match of the Day' seems almost too prophetic. Later, it evolved into a song called 'Boyfriend', which Jayne Casey used to sing. Bill wrote some words for it. It went something like, 'All those boogie rhythms start to sound the same / Are all those vodka and limes just money down the drain? / I really need a boyfriend.'

When asked if I wanted to do the England song, my initial response was, 'Not really, no.' I had no ambition to write a football record, they'd all been pretty crap beforehand.

I know everyone says the New Order one was good and to be fair, I did like it when it came out – I was swept up in all the excitement around the Italia 90 World Cup. But when I hear it now, that chant of 'Eng-gur-lun!' doesn't sit well with me. At the time there was still a strong far right element in the crowds for England. You'd go to a game and see all these openly Nazi guys supporting them. There was a lot of out-and-out racism about – if you went to Liverpool matches back then, you couldn't fail to see how John Barnes was treated for being black. It was really ugly. If anything, I was more of an Ireland fan than an England fan because there were a lot of Liverpool players in the Irish team and I really liked what Jack Charlton was doing with them. England seemed a bit yobby in comparison. I think a lot of people in Liverpool thought the same way – rightly or wrongly, we see ourselves as from Liverpool, not from England, like it's a place apart.

When the FA first asked, I hadn't really taken it on board that Euro 96 was going to be in England. Then I started seeing the posters going up around town. They were advertising that Italy were going to be playing the Czech Republic at Anfield and that really brought it home. There hadn't been a major competition here since 1966 and this was thirty years later. That was a big part of it – it's coming here, it's coming home. I could feel myself getting excited for it.

I started thinking about why I wasn't keen to do the song. I realised that I didn't like how triumphant all those songs were – they were all about how the team was great and how they were going to beat everyone. That was nothing like my experience of watching football at all. It's usually more like communal torture, with brief flashes of hope. Then I watched *Fantasy Football* on the television, presented by David Baddiel and Frank Skinner. This was different to all the other football coverage because it felt like it came from a genuine fan perspective. I thought, 'This is the attitude the song should have.' I didn't want to do a song that had the team on it, singing or rapping. I wanted a song that was from the perspective of the fans – a song that we sing and which is about how we feel.

I rang my manager back. I told him that I'd been thinking about the football song and that really, they should ask Frank Skinner and David Baddiel to do it. He asked if I knew them. 'No, I've never met them in my life,' I replied. 'I just think they'd be good.' So he went off and got in touch and asked if they would be interested. They said, 'If Ian writes the music and we can write the words ourselves, then we'd be up for it.' That worked for me because I'm not sure I could write lyrics about football. That's not the type of lyricist I am.

The plan was that they'd come up to Liverpool to meet me, but David didn't come because Chelsea were playing at home and Frank couldn't get there until late in the day. We went to Anfield first to watch Liverpool v. Leeds and then we went to my studio. It was quite late by the time we got there, maybe nine or ten at night, and it was dark. As I said, this was quite a daunting area – I think Frank was a bit worried.

There was a piano in the studio and I showed Frank this idea I had for a tune which I'd had knocking round for a while. I think we had the idea of it coming home already – the sentiment, if not the exact words. The slogan on the Euro 96 posters was 'Football comes home', so it was a reworking of that. I remember me bashing away at the piano and the two of us singing, 'it's coming back, it's coming home', or words vaguely around that theme. It didn't seem like a big deal or anything. We were still trying to work out if we should do it. I hummed the rest of the melody for Frank and we recorded it roughly on a cassette. We talked a bit about how it mustn't become this nationalistic thing. Then he took the cassette away for him and David to work on.

Soon after that I got a fax through with their lyrics. I thought they were great. They had got it exactly right. Comedians tend to be clever bastards – they are careful with words and they know the impact they have. The only thing that I didn't understand was that the words on the fax read 'Three lines'. I thought, 'I don't know what they mean by that. Is it an Adidas thing, or is it some cocaine gag?' It was the mid-'90s, so who knows? I phoned them back and asked what the 'three lines' bit meant. It turned out that they had dictated the words to someone else to write down. That person had misheard and put 'three lines'.

That's an indication of how few people knew back then that the England team had a crest on their shirts with these lions on. Even I didn't know that at the time and I thought I knew my football. After David and Frank explained to me that it was 'lions' and not 'lines', I said, 'Oh, are there lions on the shirt?' That sounds mad now. After the song, every-one seems to think that this was something that everyone always knew, but it wasn't. Nobody really referenced it. The cover of the CD single was a photo of the crest with the lions to help explain the title. Nowadays, people call the women's team the Lionesses and everybody understands why.

I recorded the music in Liverpool and then went down to Church Studio in north London, which is Dave Stewart's studio, to record the vocals. Some people can be a bit sniffy about Frank and David's vocals because they are not profes-sional singers, but I really like what they did. They inhabit that record in a way that is perfect. Sometimes a vocal is a bit like being in a film, in that it's the casting that makes it good. If you had someone like Aretha Franklin or one of the best singers in the world on that record, it just wouldn't work – it would be horrible. Frank sounds like he could be singing the *Dad's Army* theme, he has this chirpy English quaintness. David sounds just right for a football record – David's vocal really is 'Three Lions' to me. It's the icing on the cake. I think their vocals are perfect.

I finished mixing the song in my studio and I was really pleased with it. I thought it was a good tune and that their lyrics were great, but then we sent it to the FA and they really didn't like it. They thought it was too negative and they weren't happy about it not having any members of the team on it; they asked me to take Frank and David off the record. They wanted me to call the song 'The Beautiful Game' and write a new lyric around that title which members of the team could then sing. This, incidentally, was from a guy at the FA who I've since seen doing interviews where he takes full credit for the success of 'Three Lions'. He said if I did all that, then they'd be happy for it to be released as the official song. 'Fuck that,' I thought.

We told them that we'd release the record ourselves as an unofficial thing. That worried the FA because then it would have become competition and they would have had to come up with something better. They relented and said it could be released as the official song if we made some changes to the lyrics. For example, in the first verse, the original line was 'They don't know how to play', but they wanted that changed to 'But I know they can play'. We made their changes, but even so they were still a bit weird about the finished song. To this day, I'm still not sure if they're happy about it. At matches now they always play 'Sweet Caroline' by Neil Diamond and not 'Three Lions'. It's a great song, but it has nothing to do with the English team. Emotionally, it's really connected to the Boston Red Sox.

The next thing was that the FA asked us to go to Bisham Abbey, the England training camp, and play the song to the team. The vibe within the team in those days was that they didn't like the FA. The FA had them signing footballs all day long and other boring promotional jobs. When the FA asked them to do stuff, they didn't really want to do it. We arrived and were taken to meet the team in the canteen, but they really weren't that interested or friendly. Luckily, I'd met some of the Liverpool players before, people like Robbie Fowler, Steve McManaman and Jamie Redknapp, so that helped a bit. We told them we'd done this song and were going to play it for them, but I couldn't see what to play it on. They said that they'd pipe it through the muzak system used for announcements around the building. I was trying to talk them out of that as I knew how bad it would sound when Paul Gascoigne went off to get a ghetto blaster from his room.

I don't know what they were expecting, but most football songs were about how great the team were, so I assume it was probably something with that sort of lavish praise. We played the CD on Gazza's stereo and they sat there and listened. The lyrics are all about how we know they are going to lose because that's what they always do. They were a bit unimpressed by this, to say the least. The song is saying that everyone knows the score, we've seen it all before, we're gonna fucking blow it. Obviously, if you were the team, you wouldn't instantly be up for that. They were sitting in this canteen glaring at this ghetto blaster, thinking, 'What the fuck?' The most positive response we got was from Terry Venables. The England manager listened to it, then he looked up and smiled and said, 'It's a real key-tapper, isn't it?'

At this point, Frank stood up and he basically gave a speech about what the song was saying and where it was coming from. He talked about how the song reflected the fan experience, which was based on loving the team, but which was also about being burnt time and time again. In spite of all that, he said, the fans were with them and that's what we had captured in the song. It was a brilliant speech, totally off the cuff and passionate, and it won them all around. A bunch of players were up for appearing in the video after that.

Filming the bits of that video with the team in the park was such a good day. It was a bit like the calm before the storm, really, because we didn't know then that the song was going to take off like it did. It could have all gone nowhere, but that wouldn't have mattered because I would still have had that day.

The song came out and it immediately went to number one in the UK chart. Obviously as a musician I'd long fantasised about what it would be like to be number one and it turned out that, yes, it was a really great feeling. I'd recommend it. This was before the tournament had started and the country was hyped up, so the song got there on its own merits. The next week it was knocked off the top by 'Killing Me Softly' by the Fugees. A few weeks after that, we knocked them off the top and went back to number one. Then they knocked us off again, so this mad tussle was going on for the top spot that summer. It was really exciting.

But really, the charts only tell half the story of what happened with that song. It just grew and became something unlike anything I'd ever seen before. Or since. I'll always remember being at Wembley for the Holland game when the crowd spontaneously started singing it. I was like, 'Fucking hell! This is great.' Crowds never sing the official football songs; it just doesn't happen. Yet there they were, belting it out. Seventy-five thousand people had spontaneously started singing our song. After we won, they played the record over the PA and the whole stadium was singing along and they knew all the words to all the verses. And because we'd just beat Holland, there was so much joy in everyone's voices. This kept happening match after match, around the whole country. It really did feel like everywhere you went, everyone in the country was singing it.

It was crazy, all the things that happened. One of the tabloids printed the lyrics on their front page and called it the unofficial English national anthem. They started playing the record before the kick-off. It was such a great summer, it was really hot. It's such a golden memory. Me, David and Frank have all been reduced to tears by the thought of it. It did feel like we were under a spell.

It was all tied up in belief. I think the song went some way to making people believe that we were going to win. When Germany finally beat us on penalties in the semi-finals, it was crushing. But weirdly, the song was also a hit in Germany. David and Frank went over to Frankfurt and sang the song on German TV's *Football Review of the Year* programme. After Germany won the final and took the trophy home, the German team appeared on a balcony for an official celebration and they started singing the song as well. I may be wrong, but I don't think they were doing it to take the piss or rub it in, I think they genuinely liked it.

I'd spent my life writing songs that tried to capture a moment, or to preserve a moment before it was lost. Now I had written something which created its own moment. It was a very strange feeling. It felt so tied up with that golden summer that if you'd told me it would go back to number one over twenty years later, I would have thought that was insane. It's made it to number one four times now, which is something that no other record has ever done. Wherever I go in this country, I can look out at the crowds in the streets and know that pretty much everyone I can see knows a song that I wrote. I don't know if there's a songwriter alive who wouldn't swap all their music industry awards and glowing reviews to have that feeling. Is there anything better than that?

Although I wouldn't swap what happened for the world, what happened *was* complicated and it had odd consequences. Historians have started writing about 'Three Lions' as something that crystallised the moment when England regained a sense of its own identity. When you look back at the crowds in the 1966 World Cup, they are all waving Union Jacks. At Euro 96, you started to see the cross of St George. That's quite a heavy thing to put onto a football song that was intentionally not triumphant. It doesn't take much to take that attitude of hope and belief and twist it into something horrible. For example, ahead of England's semi-final against Germany, when we were knocked out on penalties, the *Daily Mirror* had this woefully embarrassing front cover. It featured mocked-up pictures of Gazza and Stuart Pearce wearing Second World War helmets with the headline, 'Achtung! Surrender! For You Fritz, ze Euro 96 Championship is Over!' Lots of people lost their minds over Euro 96 and things like that are England at its worst. I see 'Three Lions' as a very different thing to all that, but I know not everyone makes that distinction.

'Three Lions' had a negative effect on my career, to a degree. At the time, the *Jollification* album was still doing well. We were seen as a left-field indie band and that made sense in the Britpop era. Then 'Three Lions' came out and we suddenly found ourselves being lifted out of our indie ghetto and plonked down as close to the mainstream middle as you can get. For many in the music industry, this was an unforgivable crime. Our page was ripped out of the hipster bible for that unforgiveable transgression.

People who got into the band with the first couple of albums, when it was much more of a niche thing, tended to relate to those songs in a very personal way. That relationship could be quite a private and intimate thing: they saw us as their band. When we suddenly became something that everybody knew, something was lost along the way. 'Three Lions' made the Lightning Seeds incredibly famous, but it also made our album sales go down. It also overshadows the rest of the music I have made. Nowadays, if someone makes a documentary about the Britpop era, they'll talk about 'Three Lions' but all the other Lightning Seeds songs will be overlooked.

We had a tour booked that autumn in support of *Jollification*. I thought, 'Should I play "Three Lions"?', and I decided that it wouldn't be the right thing to do. It was a football song and that was a separate thing, and Frank Skinner and David Baddiel weren't around. The championship was over. I didn't want the future of the band to be overshadowed by the song. I thought about New Order and how nobody expected them to play 'World in Motion'. So we worked up a setlist without it.

The first gig was in a theatre in Preston. There were about 3,500 people there. We went on stage and I looked out and across the whole front rows were kids and their dads in England shirts. Afterwards, people would come up and say that these kids were crying because we didn't play 'Three Lions'. I just felt horrible, I didn't know what the right thing to do was. People were really angry with me for not playing it. The song became a real issue. But, at the same time, a Lightning Seeds show is about uplifting psychedelic pop and a football song doesn't really fit well there. I tried doing it, not doing it, doing an acoustic version – I tried everything, but whatever I did always felt uncomfortable in some way. I remember going through a period where I wouldn't do it and then I heard that Robbie Williams was doing it at his gigs – he had no problems with it. I, in contrast, was constantly angst-ridden about the whole thing.

Nowadays, it's different. After 'Three Lions' went back to number one following England's strong start to Euro 2020, it just seemed as if the song was everyone's property. There were all these memes around it and it sort of belonged to the world at that point. It feels easier to play now, although, when we do it, we do it at the very end of the encores. In that way, if somebody wants a 'pure' Lightning Seeds gig, they can have that – so long as they leave right before the end.

18

'BORIS THE SPIDER'

The thing that convinced me to move down to London from Liverpool after *Jollification* was a studio on a barge on the river Thames, near the bridge at Twickenham. It was an amazing place, that barge, an idyllic place to work and think and to just spend time on. It was next to Eel Pie Island, which was a big part of the jazz and blues scene in the '60s. Bands such as the Rolling Stones, Pink Floyd and the Yardbirds used to play there, so it was rich in music history. The barge was moored up outside Pete Townshend's Eel Pie Studios, which was the building where the Bella Union label was formed by Simon and Robin from the Cocteau Twins. The barge used to get its power from them. They had their own studio in that building and from the river you could look up and see the Cocteau Twins on their balcony.

There was one problem though. You were out in nature, which in theory is great. But I like to work at night, so it would be dark when I'd come along the towpath by the river to get to my studio. When I reached the gangplank to get onto the barge, a security light would come on so that I could see what I was doing. That light would come on and I'd look down at the gangplank and it would be covered in all these massive spiders. The light attracted all the flies from the river and lots of flies meant lots of spiders. There'd be literally hundreds of them, real big ones, maybe three or four inches across, freaking out in the sudden light. The gangplank would be thick with webs. I'd have to try to break the webs and knock the spiders away with a big stick to get onto the barge. They would be scuttling away towards the boat. There were just too many of them to keep track of.

I'm not good with spiders. It became this really big issue that I couldn't get onto the boat and get to work, because there were so many spiders. I obviously didn't want to kill them, so I got these people to come with a giant hose and hose the barge down. When they'd hose underneath the rim of the boat, they would knock out thousands of spiders – literally, thousands of them. They'd be coming off in this thick jet of black spidery water that was flowing into the river and people along the towpath would stop and watch as this was happening because nobody could really believe it. It was like something from a horror film. After a couple of weeks, all the spiders would be back again.

The barge studio came about through Pete Townshend from the Who. After Big in Japan split, I was in a band called Original Mirrors for a while. It was probably my least-finest hour, musically, but one amazing thing did come of it. I remember we were playing the Marquee club in Wardour Street, London, and there was this guy near the front of the audience just going mad. He was really into what we were doing. I looked at him and I thought, 'I'm sure that's Pete Townshend.' And sure enough, he came backstage and visited us in the dressing room and it was Pete Townshend. For some reason, this absolute icon was a massive fan of our band – he even had an Original Mirrors T-shirt. The weirdest thing was, this great guitar god was really into my guitar playing. He was very complimentary about it and about what I was doing. It seemed unreal, partly because I wasn't that into what I was doing myself and mainly because it was Pete Townshend of all people who was saying those things.

It was around that time I was also producing the Bunnymen. Pete liked what I was doing with that and he kept saying to me that I should produce an album of his.

I was a little intimidated and it didn't happen, but it was still an amazing thing for a young musician – to get that sense of recognition from an icon.

About a decade later, the idea of making a record came around again. We talked seriously about working together, and I told him – a bit cheekily, in retrospect – that what I really loved was the early Who stuff, before it started to get quite macho around the *Who's Next* album. I wanted to do something with a similar feel. Luckily, he liked this idea and talked about playing a Rickenbacker guitar on the album, to get those sorts of tones into it.

He had put some recording equipment into this barge by this time and the idea was that we'd use the boat as a rudimentary studio and record in this confined space – to create limitations for ourselves and create a quite simple, song-based record. The barge was coming along and all was going well. 'This will be great!' I thought. 'I'm going to make a Pete Townshend album!' Then I got a call from Pete's assistant. They said, 'Pete's fallen off his bike and broken his hand. He can't play the guitar. But he wants to carry on and do the album. Could you get another guitarist to play instead of him?'

Obviously, I had to say no. That wouldn't work. If it's a Pete Townshend album, you need Pete playing the guitar, there's no getting round it. A lot of producing is being clear about what is right and what isn't and proceeding from that. Sometimes you might really want something to work, but you have to look past that. Either it works or it doesn't. As much as I would have loved to have made that record with Pete, ultimately his busted hand meant that I shouldn't.

After his hand recovered, he put his solo career aside and started touring again with the Who and I stopped producing to commit to the Lightning Seeds, so our record together never happened. But by then the barge was kitted out and I really liked the space. I asked Pete if I could rent it off him and use it as my own studio. He kindly agreed and I rented it off him for seven years.

One of the first things I did was to finish the mix of 'Three Lions' there before working on *Dizzy Heights* (1996). I mixed the first Coral album on that barge as well. I've got a lot of great memories of the place. In many ways, it feels like the whole thing was too good to be true – being out there in nature, working on my own music and working with other bands. And yet, there were all those spiders. Even when you're in paradise, you still get the spiders.

19

'YOU'LL NEVER WALK ALONE'

I was out in America when the Hillsborough Stadium disaster happened, otherwise I might well have been at that match. This was 1989, so when you were abroad you were quite cut off from what was happening at home. I was working at Cherokee Studios in LA for a few months and there was a big newsstand that used to stock British newspapers on one of the roads nearby. Every week or so I would head down there and catch up on the news from home. The papers were usually a day old, so there was a bit of a lag between things happening and me finding out.

The British papers that particular week were a sea of red, with pictures of scarves and flowers and Anfield. I felt my blood run cold. Becky and I parked the car and went to the newsstand and that was how we found out what had happened. I then had to find a phone to call home, to check that my dad was okay. Luckily, he hadn't gone to the match, but he was still in shock because so many people that he knew had. I was sat on the side of the road in the hot California sun, reading about what happened and crying.

It had been an FA Cup semi-final, so it was an important match. The game was Liverpool v. Nottingham Forest and it was held in Sheffield as a neutral venue. It's quite easy to get to Sheffield from Liverpool, so you can see why so many supporters travelled to the game. I didn't tend to go to a lot of away matches because it's the magic of Anfield that I love. There is something romantic for me about being at that stadium. But it was the kind of big game that I would have been tempted to attend, if I'd been at home.

The first thing that hit everyone in Liverpool was shock. Ninety-four people were killed on the day and the death toll has since risen to ninety-seven. On top of that, 766 people were injured. Then there was the trauma that the rest of the crowd suffered and in a lot of cases are still suffering. To be in a crush like that, unable to move or escape, while people around you are dying is not something you're going to get over easily. In Liverpool, it felt like everyone knew someone who had been there or who had been bereaved.

By 1997, it was clear that the families still had a long and complicated legal battle ahead. They were going to need money to fund the protracted enquiry, which had been rumbling on for over seven years by that point. This led to a plan to put on a concert at Anfield, in order to raise funds to help fund the case.

There had never been a stadium show at Anfield before and there was only a narrow window to get the gig together in the preseason, so that the pitch would be okay again in time for the first game. There were a lot of hurdles to overcome, including some insurance problems which looked like they might scupper the whole thing. Fortunately, many people stepped up and gave their time and efforts to make the concert happen. Richard Branson came forward and said that he would underwrite the insurance, if we would add a band to the bill that he had just signed to his new V2 label. That band was the Stereophonics. We didn't know them at the time, but ultimately that worked out well. Most of the other bands were people I had worked with or had some connection to, like the Manic Street Preachers. I'd been writing with Nicky Wire from the Manics, and Sean Moore the drummer was a Liverpool fan. The Beautiful South, Space, Smaller and Dodgy all agreed to play. John Peel came along as well – he was our MC. The Bootleg Beatles opened the show.

When we talk about Hillsborough now, we can legally say that people had been killed unlawfully. At the time, however, the courts had not yet stated that it was unlawful. That was what Anne Williams and the Hillsborough Justice movement were pushing for with their legal challenges. In Liverpool, everyone knew that there had been a great injustice, but a lot of other people were wary about being involved.

There were two weeks to go before this massive stadium gig, and unfortunately we had no drummer. I knew that Dodgy were going to be on the bill, so I asked their drummer Mathew Priest if he would fill in for us on the night. He agreed – despite the fact that he was on tour in Australia. We had to get him a flight back from Oz a day earlier than the rest of the band for a day's rehearsal in London. He had to learn all the songs from scratch in twenty-four hours. For me, going on stage in front of a stadium crowd that size with a drummer you've never played with was very daunting, if not terrifying.

The LightnIng Seeds were the headline act, and I wanted our set to be special. Frank Skinner came along to help me sing 'Three Lions'. I doubt he'll ever forget that experience. Terry Hall also came, and he sang 'Sense'. Terry was a Manchester United supporter, so to turn up in support of Liverpool was not an easy thing for him. Fortunately, he understood that there was something bigger and more important at stake. It was a very emotional gig from start to finish and it was wonderful when Holly Johnson joined us to sing 'Ferry Cross the Mersey', which is a song he covered on the first Frankie Goes to Hollywood album, *Welcome to the Pleasuredome* (1984). He gave a magical performance.

When we were rehearsing before the big day, the band were really looking forward to Holly arriving, because they were fans but they had never met him. We were all there practising away when the doors of the rehearsal room burst open and Holly came flying in – he was out of control on his new roller skates. He went careering across the room at some speed but managed to grab onto the speakers and just stop himself from crashing into the drum kit. 'This is Holly,' I said. It was quite an entrance!

On the day, he came out in this immaculate suit with shirt and silk tie and sunglasses. He went to the mic and dedicated the song to 'everyone who has ever walked down Hope Street'. Both me and Holly have lived on Hope Street at various times and everyone in Liverpool has walked down there, but it was also a red-light area, so there was a bit of a double meaning. You can probably imagine how emotional it was for him to sing that song in front of that crowd at that location. Holly was such a star that day and a little part of me was thinking, 'This is a Big in Japan mini-reunion – and it's a stadium gig.' I realise that I was probably the only person who saw it in those terms, but it still made me chuckle nonetheless!

After our set, John Peel introduced Trevor Hicks, the chairman of the Hillsborough Families Support Group, to the stage. Trevor had lost his two teenage daughters in the tragedy and he brought the day back to being about those who had been lost and the legal fight for justice that was going to continue. Then everyone involved came back onto the stage, along with the families of the victims and a choir. We finished the day by singing 'You'll Never Walk Alone'. All around, people were in tears, just from the emotion of the day and that song.

The concert raised over 500 grand. This allowed the legal fight to go on, so it was a success in those terms. But it helped on another level as well, I think. When football and music meet, they meet on the level of community. Liverpool was broken by the tragedy and it could only be slowly healed by the community coming together and supporting each other. Among the tears of those 35,000 people singing 'You'll Never Walk Alone', that's what was happening. In that witches' brew of emotions, wounds, injustice, grief, community and music, a step towards healing was taken.

I'll never forget that day.

20

DIZZY HEIGHTS

I was very proud of the *Dizzy Heights* album. I still think it might be the best Lightning Seeds record – I started with a clear vision of what I was trying to do and I think that I managed to capture it. I started that album in Liverpool and finished it just after I had moved into my studio on the barge on the river Thames. The whole experience was a positive one for me. After *Dizzy Heights* was released and promoted, I was left with the question of what it was that I should do next.

Jollification and *Dizzy Heights* had made sense in the mid-'90s, but the musical landscape was already starting to change. The Britpop hangover had begun: the music of the biggest bands of the day had gone from bright and energetic to troubled or bloated. There was also a gulf developing between indie and pop, in which indie became anthemic but less playful, while pop became unapologetically shinier and less nuanced. The listening public seemed to split and choose a side. There was an audience for bands like Coldplay and for bands like Steps, but there didn't seem to be an audience for music that sat in the middle of them any more. This was bad news for the Lightning Seeds.

Having grown up on the Beatles and Bowie, my feeling was that I had to do something different. It felt like it was time for the costume change, the new direction, or the brave new era. I worried that people would be bored if I gave them another album that sounded pretty much like the earlier ones. As an older and wiser person now, I realise that I was wrong about this. What people really want is more of the same – they don't want you to change. If they go out and buy a Lightning Seeds album, they want it to be a Lightning Seeds album, just make it a good one.

Regardless of whether this was right or wrong, the way I went about evolving was a big mistake. I was trying to change when I didn't have a vision of what I wanted to change into. Bowie and the Beatles didn't keep changing out of fear of staying relevant. They kept changing because they had all these amazing ideas and were excited to see if they could pull them off. It's true that they didn't want to repeat themselves, but they had also come up with some new territory to explore and that's what made repeating themselves seem uninteresting. I could see glimpses of what I wanted to do differently and sometimes that can be enough to start you off. But I didn't have a complete vision in my head when I started in the way that I did with *Jollification* or *Dizzy Heights*.

When you were on a major label like Sony in the late '90s, there were all these people around who were quite prepared to tell you how you should dress and what your album should look like. Pop stars all had stylists picking out their clothes for them, hairdressers choosing their haircuts and designers coming up with record sleeves, so that they didn't have to. These were experienced professionals and in theory, they were good and knew what they were doing. There was less of this in the '70s and '80s, which I think is why bands from those days look so distinctive. They didn't really know the nuances and intricacies of style, like people would today. Instead, they just rummaged through jumble sales and charity shops hoping to find something a bit mad that would help them stand out. There was an honesty in this. Because all the clothes and hair and gimmicks came from the musicians themselves, it fitted with the music and what they were trying to express about who they were. A stylist might stop you from looking too rubbish and they might be able to dress you in a way that appeals to a certain demographic, but they also don't know you from Adam. Whatever they made you look like, it wasn't really you. It was like being a little kid, when your mum used to dress you up and try to make you look nice when you went out.

I think I understood all this at the time, but I also felt that if this was where the industry was going, then I should follow suit to fit in. I was in my early forties, so I needed all the help fitting in that I could get. No longer the penniless indie kid of the early '80s who did everything himself because he had no other option, I was now a major label pop star in the late '90s and there were people who wanted to help me. I decided to let everybody in and let them have their say.

I consciously became less of a control freak, I sat back on the production a little bit more. When other people wanted to use more synths, I agreed, even when it wasn't my instinct to do so. I went with the flow on decisions that I knew were wrong. If you listen to a song like 'Happy Satellite', for example, the great strength is its lyric. It's obvious that to do that song right, you need to be able to hear the words. In the finished version, however, the vocals are pretty buried. I knew that was wrong at the time, but still I went with it.

I'd say that my previous albums were about 99 per cent me. There would be backing vocalists and the odd extra musician coming in for specific parts, but I was still making the decisions and deciding what we should do. My engineer Cenzo Townshend was a huge help, but we were so close when we worked together that he knew exactly what I wanted. He was like an extension of me. This is why he's so brilliant at his job. With *Dizzy Heights*, I let the band in a little more, but it was still mainly me. Come *Tilt*, however, it was totally different. The band would do things like jam in the studio to see what we could come up with – this was not like me at all.

This sitting back happened across every level of the project. For promo videos, my attitude was that they should treat me like I was Robbie Williams or Atomic Kitten. They could do what they thought best and I would go along with it. The cover of the album is another example. It has a red splodge on a blue background. I'd always thought that the splodge was a kid on a bike, but now I look at it again it seems to have a tail, so maybe it is supposed to be a devil? I don't know what it's supposed to be, if I'm honest, but it doesn't look like a Lightning Seeds album.

Perhaps if the project had worked, it would have become iconic. It could have become what people thought of when they thought of the Lightning Seeds. But it wasn't meant to be. It didn't have that sense of vision around which everything could coalesce and support. All the skills of all those other creative people could have supported a brilliant piece of work, but that never happened because at the heart of it something was missing: that thing was me. I was taking a back seat on this one, but it's not a good idea to do that when you're the leader of the band.

That's not to say that I was cruising – at least, not when it came to the songs. I still sweated blood over them as I always had. I pride myself that, for all that I shake my head in bafflement at the intergalactic theatrics of the 'Life's Too Short' video, the song itself is still really cool. There was some good work on there, but there was no real sense of direction to it. The album was searching for an overall identity and I had failed to give it that.

When the album stiffed, it seemed like a natural end to the Lightning Seeds. It wasn't necessarily a sad thing. My time had come and gone. I had had a vision of what I was trying to do and I achieved that, on *Jollification* and *Dizzy Heights* at least. If I never did anything ever again, I would still have those albums. 'Three Lions' had knocked me off course and the mainstream was far from my natural habitat. It wasn't that I had a burning sense of what I had to do next and that people were preventing me from realising that. Instead, there did not seem to be anything left to do. Everything has an end.

Looking back, I think there are some great moments on *Tilt*, but I didn't quite have the energy needed to get it where it needed to go. It seemed as if the time to stop being the Lightning Seeds had arrived.

21

'SHUT THE FUCK UP!'

The keyboard player in the Lightning Seeds during the '90s was Angie Pollock. She has also played with Terry Hall and a bunch of other people, including Peter Gabriel. One day in 2011 she said, 'Peter Gabriel is doing a gig near where you live with a full orchestra at Hammersmith Apollo. I'm on the guest list, do you want to be my plus one?'

We got there and took our seats on the balcony. It was a very impressive gig and Angie loved it. She kept leaning over to tell me stuff about the music – which bits she'd played on or sung, how they'd changed it for the orchestra and details like that. It was really interesting to hear the music and her insights into it as well.

I have to stress here that neither of us was being overly loud. It was a gig. People scream and shout and cheer at gigs. They're so loud that you have to speak into each other's ear to be heard. Saying a few things to the person you're with at a gig is not a problem. I mention this because a guy sitting in front of us turned around and shouted, 'Would you shut the fuck up?'

It turned into a very ugly scene. I told him to calm himself down. I couldn't understand why he was behaving as he was – overly aggressive and oversensitive. It was a gig, you don't have to sit in silence, it's not the opera. He kept giving me this really weird look, like there was clearly some other issue. Despite the fact that it was Angie who had been talking, it was me who took the brunt of his anger. Soon we were arguing and shouting at each other. It almost got physical, although he was only a little guy and I'm only a little guy too. If we'd had handbags, we'd have been whacking each other with them.

Other people got involved. They started telling us to 'Shut up!' This just made him worse. I was trying to explain to these other people that we weren't making a noise – the noise was this guy shouting at us. Security came over and there was a big kerfuffle. A woman over to one side joined in and had a go at this guy. She was saying that it was a gig, and that I was allowed to make a noise if I wanted to. She was on my side, but she really wasn't helping. I wasn't making a noise! But by then there was such a fuss that I doubt anyone was listening to me. The gig finished and we left straight away. It was horrible, really. And quite upsetting.

I kept thinking about how the guy had seemed to recognise me. It was as if he thought, 'I'm going to have a go at him because he's famous.' This was something that I had struggled with since 'Three Lions' blew up. When I went out, people would look at me in a way that was strange and unnatural. You could never really tell what they were thinking. I don't want to seem like I'm complaining about fame here. If fame is the price you pay to make music and get your music out there where others can hear it, then I'm happy to pay that price. But at the same time, I don't enjoy it. Other people do – some people really want it and some people really get off on it. Then there are people, like my old pal Pete Burns, who are so *extraordinary* that they really should be famous. It wouldn't make any sense if they weren't. Good luck to all those people, but that's not me. I find it quite unsettling.

When I started out in Big in Japan, I went from being an unknown to being known. Or at least, in the small world of Eric's, people knew who I was. After I produced the Bunnymen album, people in the industry started to know me, or at least know *of* me. That was alright – it's nice being recognised for doing something that you are proud of. After I'd started the Lightning Seeds, I'd be recognised in indie clubs and things like that. With *Jollification*, I made a commitment to give my all to the Lightning Seeds. I was uncomfortable with that, but I forced myself to do it. In my mind I was always the guy standing off to the side playing the guitar. I always thought of myself as the organ grinder, not the monkey. When that album started to take off, the way people behaved around me started to change. It was a funny time. People would say 'hi' to you in the streets and you wouldn't be sure if it was someone you knew but couldn't place or if you were just someone they recognised. You could be talking to them for five minutes before you realised that you'd got it wrong.

You can start to become paranoid. People are friendly not because you're becoming mates in a natural way, but just because they recognise you. Sometimes it's cool and sometimes it's not, but the problem is that it's beyond your control. Even though I'm quite nondescript and the amount of fame I had compared to, say, Paul McCartney, was tiny, it was still enough to put me out of sync with normal life. The issue of what people wanted from me became a continuous worry.

The big shift for me was when 'Three Lions' came out in 1996. Before then, I'd be recognised if I went to a gig in an indie place, but not when I visited a McDonald's. After 'Three Lions', I was McDonald's Famous, for a while at least. Being recognised was something that you couldn't turn off. If you have an ongoing background sense of being under threat like I do, then people staring at you and muttering to each other feels sinister. I know that nine times out of ten it comes from a good place, but that's how it felt to me.

About a week after the Peter Gabriel gig, I got a call from David Baddiel. 'Hi, Ian, I don't know if you know but I'm suing *The Times* at the moment. They did an article where they claimed that I'd disrupted a Peter Gabriel gig by shouting all the way through it and heckling. It's really upsetting because I love Peter Gabriel. He's one of my great heroes. I wasn't even at the gig.' 'Ah,' I said. 'Well, here's a thing . . .'

To certain members of the public, the 'Three Lions' frontmen were often indistinguishable from each other. One amalgamous whole. On one occasion someone wound down their car window to shout 'Wanker' at me in the mistaken belief I was David Baddiel, only to apologise when he realised I *wasn't* in fact the boundary-pushing comedian. And don't get me started on the time when Ross Kemp thought I was deliberately posing as David Baddiel for a laugh to wind him up, when it was in fact the irate TV hardman's own confusion that had mixed us up in the first place. A little fame is a confusing place.

Thursday was local bands' night in Eric's Club, Liverpool, 1978. Me and Bill Drummond (KLF) on guitar, Julian Cope (Teardrop Explodes) on bass, and Pete Burns (Dead or Alive) on vocals.

Above: Big in Japan performing on Mathew Street, Liverpool, 1977.

Right: My Eric's membership card.

Eric's

Mathew Street, LIVERPOOL 2
Tel: 051 236 8301

MEMBERSHIP CARD

New Member.

Name .. Ian Broudie ....

Address ....

Signature   Signed
                   for Eric's

MEMBERS MAY SIGN IN TWO GUESTS
Valid until DECEMBER 31st 1979

Scottish Highlands tour with Echo & the Bunnymen: me, Pete de Freitas and Will Sergeant.

Les fixing my hair before we go on stage.

Making some final adjustments to Ian McCulloch's amp.

Playing guitar with the Colourfield in Coventry, 1985.

Recording the guitar on the intro of 'Pure' at Amazon Studios in Kirby, 1988.

With Becky on the set of the 'Pure' video.

First Lightning Seeds tour, co-headlining with Terry Hall, 1994.

Left and Below: Lightning Seeds' first American tour.

Shepherd's Bush Empire, 1996. The only Lightning Seeds gig where Frank and David joined us on stage to perform 'Three Lions'. Quite a night.

Me and Riley: from the back garden to a festival in Somerset.

Finishing off the lyrics for 'Song for No One' and then recording them during the sessions for my solo album, *Tales Told*, in Elevator Studios, Liverpool.

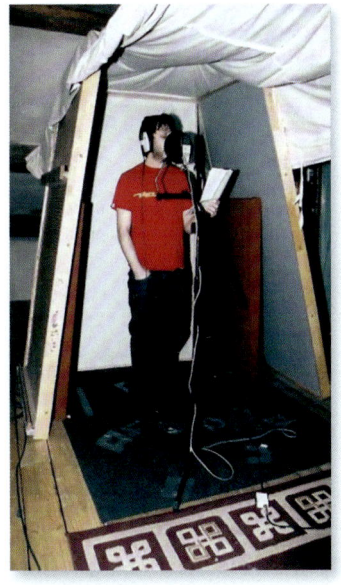

Below: One night in Hope Street with the Royal Liverpool Philharmonic Orchestra. Riley and I joined by my good friends Terry Hall (the Specials), Ian McCulloch (Echo & the Bunnymen) and Sean Payne (the Zutons).

Celebrating the twenty-fifth anniversary of *Jollification* in 2019 with a tour and a giant strawberry.

'SHUT THE FUCK UP!'

I'm pretty much resigned now to the fact that no one will ever believe me about the Peter Gabriel concert, despite *The Times* issuing a retraction. But just to be clear, one last time, for the sake of my conscience and for the sake of truth: it really was the other guy.

22

'DO YOU WANT TO COME IN?'

In the mid-'70s, a long time before I was troubled by fame, I was just this unemployed kid, one of many, who didn't know who he was or what he was going to do. I'd left school and was wandering around Mathew Street on a rainy day. That part of town was cobbled streets and old warehouses which were mainly empty. It was a rundown area of the city. There was no real reason to go there. Not any more.

I came across a building with a statue of Carl Jung in the wall. The statue was just the top half of him looking down, so it looked like Statler or Waldorf or one of the Muppets. This was a different Jung statue to the bust of Jung that is there today. Next to this building was a bit of waste ground with two giant metal containers. They were rusty and out of place and, on closer inspection, it turned out that they contained giant fridges. Inside the fridges were ice sculptures. Now, the thing with Liverpool in the '70s was that you could walk around it as much as you wanted but you were never going to find any ice sculptures, so this was very odd.

Above the statue of Jung was the name of this building – the Liverpool School of Language, Music, Dream and Pun. I stood there looking up at this mad name on the building. I looked at the statue and the ice sculptures and fridges in the waste ground next to it and I thought, 'Well, that's weird. What is this place?'

A stranger appeared at the door and invited me in for a cup of tea. I paused momentarily. Whatever was going on in that building was something different from my normal teenage life – something beyond which I had no understanding. I'd never had an invitation to the world beyond before – I think I already knew they didn't come along often. So I went in. And that seems to have been the point when my life began.

The guy's name was Peter O'Halligan, ex-Merchant Navy, aka the 'Dream Catcher' from Bootle. He was also a poet and one of those real characters who could properly tell a story. He had leased this building, and the explanation was wild. In 1927, the Swiss psychiatrist Carl Jung had a dream that completely changed his life: he dreamt he was walking through Liverpool and it was wet and miserable. He then came to a square where many roads met and he had a vision of a little island blazing with sunlight, in the centre of the square, which only he could see. In the centre of this island stood a magnolia tree in blossom and the tree was bathed in light but also at the same time it was the source of all the light. For Jung, this made Liverpool the 'Pool of Life'. He wrote in his autobiography about how this dream vision had a profound effect on him, both personally and professionally. It was a turning point in his life.

O'Halligan read Jung's account of this dream and wondered where in Liverpool it referred to. He got out a map and decided that the best candidate was the end of Mathew Street, by Rainford Square. That Jung's dream of the Pool of Life was Mathew Street where the Cavern Club used to stand, and where the Beatles emerged from, made a strange sort of sense. O'Halligan went there and he saw that this old fruit warehouse was standing empty next to the place that he thought Jung had dreamt of. Together with the Birkenhead artist and photographer Sean Halligan, he took over the building.

Now, O'Halligan just basically decided that Jung's dream was of Mathew Street. There was nothing more concrete behind it than that. But in making that decision, a whole urban myth has grown up around the place. If you go there now, there's a big mural on a building down Rainford Square with Jung's magnolia tree at the top and a walrus to represent the Beatles. It was basically one guy just making it up, but, then, isn't that how all myths and traditions start?

It turned out a guy called Ken Campbell was staging a play in there and by the time I left I was appearing in it. I would be playing the role of a guitarist in a band. The play was an adaptation of the *Illuminatus!* trilogy by Robert Anton Wilson and Robert Shea, which was this big mind-bending conspiracy epic. They had decided that it would only be worth doing if they did all three books, so the play was over eight hours long. I only had to turn up for one scene, though, so it wasn't too much of a slog for me. I was on stage with a couple of other musicians and we only had to play half a song. That was where I first met Jayne Casey.

Someone else I first encountered there was Bill Drummond. He was the set designer and stage manager and he had previously worked at the Everyman Theatre. He was five years older than me – which seemed significant at the time – and was very stern. He also played guitar in a punk band that he had just got together. They were called Big in Japan.

Just being around this production meant that I suddenly met all these mad people. It seemed as if, from that point

on, everything in the Mathew Street scene started to coalesce very quickly. Eric's nightclub started over the road
and Probe Records opened on the corner, and suddenly I
was part of this whole incredible scene of misfits and weir-
dos. There was also a little festival that they put on, called
the Mathew Street Festival. Big in Japan played as part of
it. What I mainly remember was that Charlie Alexander –
the guy who made the ice sculptures – dived off the top
of a warehouse into a vat of custard. It was dangerous as
fuck. It was unbelievable, really, but at the same time that
craziness was exactly the sort of thing that fuelled this scene
back then. And it all started because someone decided that
this overlooked forgotten little street was the place that Jung
had dreamt about in 1927.

In this troupe of actors from London were people like
Jim Broadbent, Bill Nighy and David Rappaport. When
you look at those guys now, you think, 'Wow, what a cast,'
but at the time, they were just young or youngish guys
starting out. It was all done with next to no money, but
it was all insanely ambitious too. The director was Ken
Campbell, who had these mad bushy eyebrows. He was
always smiling. He had a vision in his head and everyone
in the troupe just seemed to love and adore him. I only
knew him briefly during the show, but I remember him as
one of those guys who had extraordinary charisma.

Ken had this notion that something was only worth doing if it was impossible. There was a Japanese woman in the play, so he said to himself, 'Who's the most famous Japanese woman in the world?' He decided that it was Yoko Ono, so he got on the phone and started ringing New York, trying to get in touch with Yoko. He was acting like he was London's West End when we were all just a bunch of nobodies who had taken over an old fruit warehouse in a backstreet in Liverpool with only one bog. This attitude of his made a real impact on people. You started to think, 'What have we got to lose?' Ken's attitude helped to inspire the ambition of the Eric's scene. It was quite punk in a way, but the difference was that it wasn't 'No Future'. It was, 'Anything's Possible'. With that, the spark was lit and the street regenerated and took on a new life.

Ken's direction to Bill Drummond as he was designing and building the sets was to keep asking himself, 'Is it heroic?' So Bill wrote that phrase in big letters on the wall in the basement room he was working in. He was building these crazy sets at strange scales. They were sets for this mad epic story of global conspiracy, but they had to be tiny because otherwise he couldn't get them up the stairs from his basement workshop. The story was about Discordianism, which is either a real religion disguised as a spoof, or a spoof religion disguised as a real one, depending on who you asked. Bill would later take all those ideas and use them in his band, the KLF – the whole notion of the Justified Ancients of Mu Mu, for example, are taken from that book. Working with all these strange, nebulous ideas certainly had an effect on people. When I sing in 'The Life of Riley' about how 'it's certain nothing's certain', that's a very Discordian idea.

The fact that this scene sprang up right by the Cavern Club was quite an odd coincidence, really. There was a pub a few doors down from Eric's called the Grapes. All of us young punks would drink in there. Over on the other side of the pub there'd be all these old fellas who we didn't really pay a lot of attention to, but we were aware of. It was characters like Bob Wooler, who was the DJ at the Cavern and who John Lennon famously punched at Paul McCartney's twenty-first birthday party, and Allan Williams, the Beatles' first manager. They would be in there with all these Mersey Beat musicians who I'd love to talk to now, but at the time we were too young and wrapped up in ourselves to show any interest.

All this would have been in the mid- to late '70s, maybe 1976 or '77. It really wasn't that long after the Beatles had split up, but when you're a kid, you think of a few years like that as being an impossibly long time. If you look at this from the point of view of music history, it was just the blink of an eye, really. Yet it wasn't the case that our scene was informed by or grew out of theirs in any way. That earlier stuff was nothing to do with us – it was just a different world.

Roger Eagle, who was the DJ who set up Eric's, would say to us, 'Don't listen to the Beatles because you're not going to do that stuff better than they did. You've got to come up with your own thing. If any journalists ask you about the Beatles because you're from Liverpool, say that you hate them and you don't listen to that old crap.' Obviously, I did listen to and love the Beatles, but the Eric's thing was to pretend that you didn't. Now, I never used to go along with that because I'd loved the Beatles since I was a kid. That was something of a black mark against me in the Eric's culture of the time.

It just seems quite funny now, these two very different scenes crossing over like that, all sitting in the pub pretty much ignoring each other. I do remember Allan Williams coming over after I had joined Big in Japan and saying, 'I used to manage the Beatles, you're a band, I'll manage you.' We just said, 'No, you're okay.' But, thinking back now, the idea of Big in Japan having the same manager as the Beatles would have been something.

When I think back to all this, what strikes me is the serendipity. I was casually invited in for a cup of tea. Me! I was just some kid, and Liverpool was full of thousands of kids like me. We're not normally invited in, and we're not normally asked what it is that we can do. Normally, we're told to clear off. It was such a pivotal turning point for me that I can't imagine what my life would be like if I hadn't gone into that building that day. On one level, it seems like pure luck that I wandered down that street, but perhaps all us Eric's lot had to find each other, no matter what.

23

'LISTEN TO THIS!'

Back in the late '70s, Roger Eagle, DJ and promoter, was one of the most important people on the Liverpool music scene. A big guy who often had a moustache, he looked pretty straight – he did not look like a hipster or a music tastemaker. I think everyone who went to Eric's will agree that you can't overstate what he did for us, or for Liverpool music in general.

The first time I met him was around the time of the *Illuminatus!* play, before he started the club. He would have been in his mid-thirties at the time, which seems pretty ancient when you're seventeen. I was hanging around with a guy called Bob Bellis, who would go on to be the drummer in a band called Yachts. For a brief period before they changed their name to Yachts, the band were called Albert Dock and the Cod Fish Warriors and that's the name they had when they supported the Sex Pistols in 1976, at the original version of Eric's. Bob used to have his drums covered in fish wallpaper, of the type you would get in chip shops. You have to admit, that was a great bill – the Sex Pistols plus Albert Dock and the Cod Fish Warriors!

Bob lived in the same house as Roger, at the top of Aigburth Road. I had been aware of Roger before because he used to put on gigs in an old boxing arena called the Liverpool Stadium. He booked people like Lou Reed, Captain Beefheart and David Bowie, so he was upping the quality of music in the city from as soon as he moved to Liverpool. Before this he had been a DJ at the Twisted Wheel in Manchester and he had played an important role in the Northern Soul scene. Even though I didn't get to speak with him at that point, I think I was aware of who he was. I knew that he mattered. Going over to Bob's place, however, was the first time I sat down with him and talked.

I say we talked, but mainly what happened was that he gave me a massive spliff and said, 'Listen to this,' then put on Kraftwerk's *Autobahn*. He played it from start to finish. I had never heard anything like it before. He said, 'This will blow your mind,' and it really did. It's the perfect Roger memory, really – that was him in a nutshell. He knew everything about music and he wanted to share his knowledge as widely as he could. There was a good book written about him by Bill Sykes called *Sit Down! Listen to This!*, a title that perfectly captured Roger. Whenever I visited him, he would always lend me a couple of albums which I would never have heard otherwise. Then I'd go back to return them a few weeks later and borrow a couple more.

There was another side to my musical education, which is probably worth mentioning because, with hindsight, it was pretty odd. Back then, there used to be a Woolworths on Allerton Road. They had all the normal chart records as you might expect, but they also had another rack called 'deleted records'. These records all had the corner of the sleeve cut off, to differentiate them from the 'proper' records, and they were all marked down ridiculously cheap. The thing is though that the records in those racks are now recognised as being really important and ground-breaking albums. There was Captain Beefheart, Love, Scott Walker, the Doors, Faust and a lot of Krautrock. There was a label called Track Records, who would release sampler albums which might have the Who on one side and Jimi Hendrix on the other. You would expect these shunned albums with their corners cut off to be terrible, but they were amazing. As a kid in the days before Spotify, you desperately wanted new records and each album you owned was precious, but they were expensive. And yet, I could just go down Allerton Road Woolworths and pick these things up for about 60p. I would flick through the deleted racks and find something with a great cover and take a chance. Nowadays, if you go to the hippest vinyl record shop, they basically stock the exact same records, but they all have crazy prices. If I was getting all these obscure and eclectic records, then I suspect that other kids in Liverpool must have been doing so also. Roger's musical education was definitely central to shaping the Liverpool scene, but we shouldn't overlook the influence of the deleted section of Woolies.

Whenever a scene forms, the temptation is to look for one key person at the heart of it. The scene may be about a place or whole crowds of people, but it's easier to get a grip on something when you can focus on just one person. Sometimes there is a likely candidate who is a real self-promoter, who'll try to make it all about themselves anyway. Tony Wilson in Manchester is a good example, as was Malcolm McLaren in the London punk scene. It's very easy for the press to get their heads around people like that and use them to turn a rich and complex musical happening into a simple story. The problem is, though, that when you use those people to frame a scene, it distorts it quite a bit. The Manchester story becomes all about Tony's civic pride and the Sex Pistols become all about how clever Malcolm was and how he pulled a fast one. The actual music was so much larger and better than any of that.

I think Roger probably was the heart of the Liverpool scene, but he was concerned much more with educating people than promoting himself. He would introduce people to the best music and the implication was that this was the standard you had to aspire to. We were all young and stupid and ambitious. When all the people around you were trying to be as good as the music Roger introduced us to, then you had no choice but to aim that high as well.

Shortly after I met him, Roger opened the club Eric's, together with Ken Testi, who used to manage Deaf School, and Pete Fulwell, who went on to manage the Christians. It was originally held in a basement in Victoria Street, which is where it was when the Sex Pistols plus Albert Dock and the Cod Fish Warriors played. It very quickly moved to a basement in Mathew Street, opposite where the Cavern used to be. There was a trend at the time for naff clubs to be called after posh girl's names such as Annabel's or Tiffany's. They reacted against this by deciding to call their club Eric's.

Inside Eric's it was loud and hot and it smelled, so they got the name about right. The walls were painted red and black, the classic anarchist colours, and there were a few stools and other bits of furniture scattered around. There was a bar and a place where you could get chips, and a low stage at the end of the room. The toilets, as you can probably guess, were pretty nasty and what carpet there was stuck to your boots. But none of that mattered. It was the music you heard at Eric's that mattered and the people who came to hear it.

At one point Eric's set up their own label. They released a 7-inch split single with 'Big in Japan' by Big in Japan on one side and 'Do the Chud' by the Chuddy Nuddies on the other. The Chuddy Nuddies was briefly the name of Bob's band after they were Albert Dock and the Cod Fish Warriors and before they were Yachts. Band names were not their strong point, it's fair to say. The single was called 'Brutality, Religion and a Dance Beat' and that title came from Roger. Those were the three ingredients, he believed, that all pop music needed.

Eric's closed down in 1980. It never really recovered after the police raided it for drugs and, with the loss of that club, the focus of the whole Liverpool post-punk scene also went. I was in London when I heard it was shutting and it's hard to describe what that felt like. People know what it's like to lose a friend or to lose a pet, but to lose a club is something else. It's not something that you are prepared for: you lose a whole like-minded community. Eric's was one of those magical parts of your life that you almost took for granted while it was happening. It was so central to everything that you couldn't imagine it not being there. It was only after it was gone that you finally realised how important it had been to you.

After Eric's ended, Roger ended up living in a warehouse in a different part of Liverpool with my mate, Tim Whitaker. Tim had previously been the drummer in Deaf School, but by that point he was a struggling artist. They had no heat in this warehouse. A plug socket was coming through from somewhere, which they plugged an electric heater into, but it was a little thing that had no hope of heating up this draughty big warehouse. This was in the middle of winter and they became really ill, ending up in hospital with pleurisy. So Roger was in a pretty bad way after Eric's closed and I think he thought that he might be cracking up. What he did then was decide that Cracking Up would be his next project. He had no club and no venue or any real plan, but he had membership cards made with 'Cracking Up' written on them. He gave me one. 'What's this?' I asked. 'I don't know yet,' he replied 'but you're an honorary member.' I'm strangely proud of that – there's not many people who can show that they are an honorary member of Cracking Up.

After this, though, Roger moved back to Manchester and got another club off the ground. This was the International.

The last time I ever saw him was when I went there to see the Colourfield, which was the band that Terry Hall formed after Fun Boy Three had split. A group of us made the trip – there was me, Jayne Casey, Becky, and Biffa from the Pale Fountains. We all knew Terry from my working with him and our mate, Gary Dwyer, was his drummer.

Terry had somehow come across this young band called Happy Mondays, who he really loved. This was before my old schoolmate Nathan McGough became their manager, but I think he was already involved with them in some way because he had sent me a tape of their demos a few weeks earlier. Terry took the Mondays on tour with him. He was the first person to recognise how good they were and I think this was the first tour they did. This gig has a bit of a legend around it because Tony Wilson was there and it was the first time he saw them. Straight away, he knew he was going to sign them.

I was chatting to Shaun Ryder recently, and he was telling me that when he started out, he hadn't really figured out what a singer should be like onstage, so he watched Terry and tried to be like him. He said he probably hasn't changed his approach much since then. That's just another reason to love my mate Terry Hall.

We arrived at the club and there was Roger Eagle, in one of those mad Hawaiian shirts that he used to wear. After a bad few years, it felt like he'd found his place in the world again. He just seemed so delighted to see us all. 'It's the Eric's kids!' he kept saying, even though we were all a bit older than kids at that stage. He was as full of enthusiasm as he ever was. He said, 'I've got some lads here that you have to meet, they're such a great band,' and he took us over to meet this group that his bar manager was looking after: this was the Stone Roses.

I find it quite funny that the last time I saw him, it felt like the start of a new chapter. There he was, on his feet again, telling everyone about the great music he found and surrounded by two bands who would play such a big part in British culture in the years ahead. He was exactly where he should have been. That was the last time I saw him. He died in 1999. The first time I met him was perfect, and so was the last.

24

BIG IN JAPAN

Big in Japan weren't a band who were together long – I think we only did about fifteen gigs. People still talk about us because of what the members of the group did afterwards, rather than because of how good or bad we were. We are said to be like a supergroup in reverse. Nobody was interested in us at the time, but after we split and went our own ways, we all made a tonne of hit records. There was Holly Johnson from Frankie Goes to Hollywood on bass, Bill Drummond from the KLF on guitar, Budgie from Siouxsie and the Banshees on drums, and Jayne Casey singing. Or at least that was the line-up for a while. It did chop and change quite a bit. Dave Balfe from the Teardrop Explodes, for example, came in and replaced Holly towards the end. Among all that, there was me on guitar. After we split up, members of the band had about seven number-one singles and sixteen top-ten hits between us. That's also not including singles like 'You Spin Me Round (Like a Record)' by Pete Burns and Dead or Alive. I don't think Pete was ever technically a member of the band, but he was always around and very much part of the Eric's scene.

As mentioned, I met Bill Drummond and Jayne Casey when I played guitar in Ken Campbell's play. Bill had got Big in Japan together a few months earlier, with Clive Langer from Deaf School and a couple of others. Jayne had just joined them as their new singer. She had this really wild energy and she looked amazing with her shaved head, so it made total sense that they would want her as their frontwoman. Jayne and Bill asked me if I would join the band as a guitarist and I said yes straight away. I didn't have the mad punk energy that Jayne had, I still looked like a schoolboy really. But they knew that I could play a bit, which was unusual at the time, and 'a bit' was enough.

For a lot of people on the Eric's scene, actual musical ability was pretty secondary. Instead it was made up of a wild mish-mash of hedonists, artists, attention-seekers, misfits, outcasts and oddballs. If they were around now, a lot of them wouldn't have become musicians: they'd have become influencers. They needed someone to sort out the music while they were busy dreaming or being looked at, which is how someone like me became accepted by that crowd. We were all starring in our own fantasies and playing in a mad punk band like Big in Japan was exactly what I wanted to do at the time. I was made up that they wanted me, that I was being accepted by people like that.

The first problem was that we needed somewhere to rehearse. Jayne had a flat in Faulkner Street, so we set up in there one night and started to play. Before too long, the doorbell rang and she went to answer it. These two really big guys came in, sat down and stared at us. The room went quiet. The main one was a notorious Liverpool gangster, a really heavy character. I've seen documentaries about him since, he's quite famous in gangster circles. He was not someone that you wanted anything to do with, put it that way. It turned out that he was really not happy with us. He said, 'My mum lives in the flat below next door and you've woken her up. We're not going to hurt you now but if you ever do this again, we *will* hurt you.'

And that was my first rehearsal. A few years later, I ran into that gangster again when I was becoming known as a record producer. I was in a bar called Kirklands on Hardman Street, playing pool with Will from the Bunnymen, when this heavy came over. He said that this gentleman was over in the corner and he wanted to speak to me. I tried to get out of it, but he made it clear that this wasn't a request. He took me over to meet him: 'You're the record producer, aren't you?' I said that I was. He nodded to the heavy who had brought me over and said, 'This guy's going to drive you over to my flat. He's got the keys. My stereo is broken. I need you to go and fix it.' I pleaded that I didn't know how to fix a stereo, only to be told that I must do, because I was a record producer! In the end I said I'd pay for a new stereo because I couldn't fix one. Fortunately, that got me off the hook, and I was dismissed. That's the record producer's job in a nutshell – people are never 100 per cent sure what it is that you do.

We still needed a place to rehearse but we had heard about an arts space called the Open Eye Gallery, which was opening up on Whitechapel. They were building a little studio in there which we would record in later. Someone had discovered that there was a hatch in the floor of one of the rooms, like a trap door. If you opened that hatch, you could climb down underneath the building and there was this strange room underneath. It was like a brick cellar. We asked the gallery people if we could rehearse in that room, seeing as no one was using it. I don't think they even knew that the room was there, so they were a bit unsure about it. But they couldn't think of a reason to say no, so they agreed.

Somehow, we managed to get all our gear down there and turned it into a passable rehearsal space. We put a carpet down and ran a cable from upstairs for electricity. It looked like it was going to work out really well, so we came back again a few days later and started rehearsing. We were making our racket but quickly stopped and fell quiet at about the same time. Someone said, 'Can you hear something?' We all listened. There was a rumbling sound, like the rush of water. It was raining heavily that day and previously when we had been down there, it had been dry. There were these iron grates that led off into darkness at either end of the room, which we hadn't really paid any attention to. It turned out that the room was part of the underground overflow for the Mersey.

Panicked, we started chucking the amps up and out through this hatch above us. We were trying to get Budgie's drums up through this trap door while this roar was getting louder and louder. Just moments after the last of us got out, the water hit and the underground room was completely flooded with Mersey water. We came this close to all being drowned; we never went back down there again. We never saw that carpet again, either.

That was our second attempt at rehearsing. Amazingly, a little bit after this the gallery people let Echo & the Bunnymen use that cellar for their first rehearsal, after

Les Pattinson had joined the group – I think it was just Will and Les, as Ian didn't turn up. When they went down there, it wasn't dry like it was when we found it. There was mud and puddles all over the floor. Ever practical, Les and Will just put the amps up on chairs in an effort not to electrocute themselves and went about their business.

All of this was what led us to rehearsing in Eric's. This got me into the habit of being in the club in the day – when it was empty – as well as the night. Roger would sometimes bung me a fiver to help unload a band's gear, or to DJ, or to do whatever needed doing. Soon, Eric's became much more than just a club. It was the centre of my world, really.

Because we used to rehearse there, Big in Japan became seen as a house band. Sometimes Roger would get us a gig outside Liverpool. Bill would hire a transit van because he was the only one old enough. The idea was we'd all jump in the van and drive back the same night. There was no question of hotels or anything back then, and certainly no hope of any pay. It wasn't just the band that would go – a load of mates and Eric's regulars would get in the van and come with us. Julian Cope came a few times, as did Gary Dwyer, Pete and Lynne Burns, Paul Rutherford and Holly Johnson. Holly used to come along before he was even in the band. It was Eric's on tour, basically – we were there as a band, but we were also a representation of the club. It was a laugh and it worked well because we basically brought an audience with us. Sometimes there'd be no one else there and it was just us playing to our mates as usual, except that we'd all be in Bradford.

At that time the hunt for the Yorkshire Ripper was at its peak. This meant that if you were driving across Yorkshire in a van at night, you'd be stopped. We were stopped repeatedly – sometimes three or four times in a night. The police would open up the van because they were trying to find this serial killer and they'd find all these freaks crammed together along with guitars and amps, trying not to freeze to death in the middle of winter. What they made of that, I don't know. But it was a strange backdrop to those times – the idea that you'd go out across the country and there would be a monster out there, somewhere in the darkness. You'd play a gig and there would only be men in the audience because women were too scared to go out.

So Big in Japan had Liverpool gangsters, the Yorkshire Ripper police and the elemental force of the Mersey against us. All that makes it sound like it was your typical earnest, heavy punk vibe, but it wasn't like that at all. It wasn't a serious thing. We only had about five songs and we used to play them all a couple of times each during a gig. Not being serious was the point of it, to some extent. A lot of punk rock was a very macho thing and a lot of people were very intense about it. The music press would take bands like the Clash very seriously and write about them as being important politically. We were the opposite, a reaction against all that. Jayne Casey would come on stage with a lampshade on her head. She talked about how she wanted us to be cartoons, like the Monkees. We had a song called 'Reading the Charts', which was just Jayne reading out that week's pop charts while the rest of us improvised horrible feedback in the background. Whenever I mention that to people, they all say that they'd love to hear it. It's probably a good thing that it was never recorded. The idea of the song was much stronger than the actuality. That sums up Big in Japan pretty well: never quite as good in reality.

Bill Drummond really liked Wilko Johnson from Dr Feelgood. He decided that he wanted to be as much like him as possible. He dressed like Wilko and he tried to play the guitar like him. He tried to move like him and copy all his mannerisms. If you look at any photos of Big in Japan, Bill's always doing a hard stare or pulling a face to look like Wilko Johnson. That was his thing and we left him to it. We weren't professional enough to have a conversation about whether this was a bad idea, we all just did whatever it occurred to us to do. If I ever had to sing, I'd sing in a London accent because I thought you had to sing in a

London accent if you were punk rock. It was all very naïve but it was spontaneous and liberating.

In May 1978, Big in Japan drove over to Manchester to play a gig in the Russell Club, which was this rundown little club in Moss Side. It was surrounded by the roughest housing estates and it smelt of burgers. The reason why this is now considered significant is because the night had been put on by Tony Wilson. He called this club night 'The Factory' and this led to Factory Records, the Hacienda and the whole modern myth of the Manchester music scene.

I first met Tony due to a connection with the first band I was ever in. We were called the O'Boogie Brothers and we used to play reggae – this was back in the days before Eric's. We were mainly just a bunch of kids, so we didn't have any way of getting to gigs. My uncle and my cousin Richard used to work in a builder's yard, however, and they had a big blue open-back truck. They would slip me the keys in the evening when the yard was closed, and I'd nip in and borrow it. The back was always full of cement and builder's paraphernalia. We'd pile all the gear in there and I'd drive us all to the gig. Thankfully it never rained, but if it had, all of our equipment would have become cemented into the back of that truck.

The keyboard player was an older guy who we didn't know that well. He used to wear an old army greatcoat, and he liked a drink. He would come into rehearsals with a half-bottle of whisky in one side pocket, and a little Labrador puppy in the other. He would then put the whisky bottle on the keyboards, put the puppy behind the bass amp, and start rehearsing. The puppy seemed quite happy there, except when our bass player Ambrose hit a low E, at which point the dog would crap itself. The smell would come wafting over, and we'd all have a go at Ambrose. He then had to avoid playing that note during rehearsals. I don't think it ever occurred to us to move the poor dog. All that probably gives you an idea about how ramshackle this band was.

Probably the most noteworthy thing about the O'Boogie Brothers was that the singer was my schoolmate, Nathan McGough. His dad was the poet Roger McGough, who was a big part of that massively influential poetry anthology *The Mersey Sound*. Roger was also in a band called the Scaffold with Paul McCartney's brother, Mike. They had had a mad number one in 1968 called 'Lily the Pink', so he was quite an interesting guy on many levels. One day, I went round Nathan's house and Tony Wilson was there. This was really weird at the time because he was a reporter on *Granada Reports*, so I'd seen him on the television. It was quite an odd thing when you were a school kid to go round your mate's house and find someone off the telly in the front room. If I remember right, Tony was friends with Nathan's mum. Years later, Nathan became the manager of the Happy Mondays, so he ended up working with Tony again. I still remember being introduced to him; he was full of beans and enthusiasm. Me and Nathan were talking about our reggae band and Tony turned to me and said, 'You should be a punk band. It's going to be massive.' Those were the first words that Tony Wilson said to me. You have to admit, he wasn't wrong.

Often when people talk about the post-punk days, they see the Liverpool and Manchester scenes as being quite separate things. That wasn't how it felt at the time. We felt that we were all part of the northern alternative music scene. There weren't a lot of us, so when we met up with others, it was like there was an automatic bond there. There was a lot of back and forth along the M62 by bands from both cities, and Zoo Records and Factory Records would put on joint events. Roger Eagle had been a DJ at the Twisted Wheel in Manchester before he set up Eric's in Liverpool, so he saw no division and I don't think all us Eric's kids did either. Maybe the division came about because Tony Wilson and a few others had this weird sort of civic jingoism, which was all about Manchester being the best city on Earth. That framed their scene as a separate thing. A world apart. It wasn't quite like that in Liverpool. I don't think you'd get many who saw Liverpool as the best place on Earth. It was our favourite place, but that's a subtly different thing.

Big in Japan played the second Factory night. It was on one of those long, hot '70s summer days and we were supported by a band called Manicured Noise. This is mainly remembered now because of the poster advertising the gig. Tony had got Peter Saville, who was just an art student back then, to make a poster that advertised the first four Factory club nights at the Russell Club. It listed all the bands that would be on. In later years, I would work with Saville a fair bit. He did the sleeves for Original Mirrors' records and things like that. For this poster, Peter nicked a yellow laminated 'Use Hearing Protection' sign off the wall at Manchester Poly, which he traced and put on a bright yellow background. It was a very clean, striking image. Famously, the posters weren't done in time for the first night, which the Durutti Column played, so the first gig that they were used to advertise was the Big in Japan one.

That first Factory poster has now become legendary, mainly because Tony Wilson gave it the catalogue number FAC 1. That makes it the beginning of the Factory story and as such, it has become seen as this iconic thing. Forty-five years later and Peter was trying to find the original sign, which had been lost or stolen, to put in an archive of Manchester history. If you'd have told us back when we played that dingy old club that the poster would be in a museum in the twenty-first century, we would have thought you were mad.

One time I went to Eric's and a couple of people came up to me. They said, 'There's a bloke in here with a badge on that says, "I hate Ian Broudie".' I went searching for this guy and I found him. 'What the fuck's this?' I asked incredulously. 'I don't even know who the fuck you are.' To which Wylie retorted quite plainly, 'I should be in that band instead of you.' And that was the sole reason for the badge. There was a lot of competition and one-upmanship around the scene, but at the same time it was all quite playful. Julian Cope got a petition together for people to sign, demanding that Big in Japan split up. You could go into Probe Records and sign it, so of course everyone in the band went in and did just that. It was just funny, things like that. That was the spirit of the thing – it was all just a joke but at the same time, it was a big deal. But because it didn't matter, it somehow *really* mattered.

As a gang, we were always dreaming up new bands with exotic names and ever-changing line-ups, few of which ever went anywhere. At one point I was supposed to be in the Opium Eaters with Pete Wylie and Paul Rutherford, while Ian was meant to be in the Crucial Three with Wylie and Julian Cope. You'd be lucky if any of these pretend bands ever played a note. There was something very seductive about it though. It took courage to get on stage and be prepared to risk making a fool of yourself – it was much easier to just come up with a name and then wait for the myth to grow. When you're playing in a *Wizard of Oz* world of dreams and imagination, not everyone wants to peek out from behind the curtain and look the world in the eye.

I think we all learnt a lot. We all dreamed big dreams and in the end that's what unites all of us who were lucky enough to be part of that weird collective. I think everyone who was in that band who went on to have hits and success would credit being in Big in Japan with shaping who they were, creatively. It didn't last long and we didn't play many gigs, but each one of them was an adventure. When it threatened to get serious – that was when we stopped. It was right to stop.

At the end of it all, the band had an overdraft of about £400 and we didn't know how to pay it off. We decided we'd do two gigs at Eric's, a matinee and an evening, and we'd make a record on the four-track in the Open Eye gallery. It was all very basic, just a tape machine in a little room, that sort of thing. I don't know if you could say that I produced that record – what I did was so rudimentary that I doubt you would describe it as producing. But we recorded a couple of songs there, cobbled them together with a couple of others, and we had a four-track EP to sell. It was called *From Y to Z and Never Again* (1978). To release it, we also had to have a record label, so the band started a label which we called Zoo Records. The record got good notices in the *NME* and music press and, together with the gigs, we made enough money to pay off our overdraft and split up.

The whole point of Zoo Records was that it was only meant to release that one-off record. After we had parted ways, however, Bill Drummond and Dave Balfe, who had been filling in on bass towards the end, asked the rest of us if they could take the label over and use it to release other stuff. We all said that this was fine by us. They went on to release music by Echo & the Bunnymen and the Teardrop Explodes. Nowadays, the legend is that the label is called Zoo Records because they thought of all their bands as animals, which the label had caged and exhibited. Like a lot of the myths around the post-punk Liverpool scene, however, that's an example of coming up with a good line after the fact.

Being in Big in Japan gave me an identity, in a way. It was the first time that I felt noticed. People like Jayne, Holly, Pete Burns – they were the glitterati. They were sharp and clever, looked outstanding and they were a *gang*. And while I won't say that I was *part* of that gang, I was associated with it. To look at me, I was probably the last person you would have thought would fit in with people that glamorous. There I was with my National Health glasses and my jumper, while they looked like they'd come from outer space. But by association, I became a bit of a face in that small scene and people would know of me before they met me, which was quite an odd thing. That's what happened with Will from the Bunnymen. Before we ever met, Jayne Casey came bounding up to him in Mathew Street and said, 'Will! We've got a new guitarist! He's brilliant and he looks about twelve!'

25

'ANOTHER GIRL, ANOTHER PLANET'

Big in Japan may not have been great, but we did support some great bands. Towards the end we opened for the Only Ones, which was exciting. Afterwards, their guitarist, John Perry, came up to me in the dressing room. I was still this little scally kid and I was a bit in awe of him, but he was really kind. The Only Ones were part of that late '70s London punk scene where there was a lot of heroin flying around, which was all a bit intimidating. If you listen to a track like 'Another Girl, Another Planet', however, you can see how they were an influence on me and the Lightning Seeds.

John said, 'You're great on the guitar, I really liked what you were doing. You should really be in a better band.' I said, 'Well, we're splitting up actually. I don't know what

I'm going to do next.' He said, 'I've got friends from New York who are in London at the moment and they'd probably love you. You should go and audition for their group.' He gave me a phone number and said, 'Ask for Patti.' This was Patti Palladin, who had a group called Snatch with Judy Nylon. So I phoned up and explained how John Perry said I should get in touch. Patti said, 'We're living in Brian Eno's house in Elgin Mews in Maida Vale in London. We're going to do a record with him. Come down and meet us.' This was great, I'd somehow hit the jackpot. So, with little thought about what I'd do when I got there, I immediately headed down to London on a rainy winter's day, with just this address on a piece of paper in my pocket and nowhere to stay.

I got to the house and knocked on the door. I don't know what they were expecting but I think they were taken aback. There I was, this small, very young Scouser on their doorstep, while they were ultra-hip, leather-clad New York punks. It turned out that Judy was going out with Johnny Thunders from the New York Dolls and they were all living in this house with his band. I think this was around the time the Heartbreakers were splitting up, so he might have been putting a new band together. Johnny and his band were rehearsing somewhere when I arrived, but it was decided that when they finished, we'd go to their rehearsal room and use their equipment. I'd try out for Patti's band and they'd see what they made of me. So we sat round all day waiting. They were all very New York – unconvinced and not overly friendly, put it that way. I felt awkward and nervous.

We got to this rehearsal room quite late. It had been a long day. I got there and there was this huge stack of Marshall amps and a Flying V guitar – it was all Very Rock. So I plugged in and we started to jam a few tracks and I don't know what I did, but it seemed to fit. I was invited back to their place, which was fortunate – 'Come back to the flat and stay with us in the house.' This was ideal for me because by then it was really late, I didn't know anyone in London and I had nowhere else to stay.

We got back to the flat and I was thinking, 'This is really nice! These people are the real deal. This is going to work out well.' It was exciting because the music that I *really* loved in the punk scene was coming out of New York. I liked bands like the Clash and the Sex Pistols well enough, but really, I could take them or leave them. The bands I really loved were Talking Heads, Patti Smith, the Ramones, the Velvet Underground and, of course, the New York Dolls, so to find myself in this New York scene with Johnny Thunders was a real thrill.

But then I felt the atmosphere darken, and I noticed for the first time some drug paraphernalia dotted about.

It was scary and dark, and I was a bit shocked. I felt like I was expected to join in, and I didn't know what to do. It felt as if maybe this was as casual as having a glass of wine. Maybe it would be fun.

I needed a quick timeout to think, so I picked up my bag and went into the toilet. I shut the door and then, without thinking at all, I opened the window and climbed out. I got a bus to the motorway and hitched back to Liverpool in the middle of the night. And for all that I loved the New York punk scene, I've never regretted that decision. I felt like I'd dodged a bullet. I'm a bit of a hypochondriac, and although I understand the allure of that world, and its place in music mythology, I knew it wasn't me. That lifestyle is often romanticised as Byronic boundary-pushing aesthetes, but I've been in close proximity to that world at times and I know it's really not romantic at all.

Fast-forward a long time into the future and I went to see Blondie at the Lyceum in the '90s. I was with my friend Lee and we were all at the after-show, having a drink. This woman came up to me and said, 'Are you Ian? Ian from Liverpool?' I was like, 'Wow, it's Patti!' And she said, 'You went to the toilet twenty years ago. What the fuck happened to you?'

26

'PERMANENT DANGER'

I first met Julian Cope at Eric's. This was before he formed the Teardrop Explodes. He was there with his first wife, Kathy, and their friend Hillary, who I'm still in touch with. They were all from the teacher training college out in Ormskirk and they were all very young – although I was even younger. They were really excited to be in Eric's, I remember. Julian was a slightly posh kid from Tamworth, so Eric's was something new and exciting for him.

One day he invited me round to his for tea. This was a bit weird in itself – normally you might meet a mate for a drink and then go back and listen to records, but no one had ever invited me to tea before. Julian was already a bit different to the other people I knew because he was married, even though he was still a teenager. I didn't know anyone else our age who was married, so that in itself seemed strange. Maybe it was down to Kathy, who, unbelievably, in many ways was far weirder than Julian. She was a great eccentric, was Kathy.

I called round to their little flat at the appointed time. It was a little one-room bedsit in Edge Lane. Julian said to me, 'Look, you live at home with your mum, so you're okay for food. We're students so we're poor. So, if it's okay with you, we can't really give you any tea but we can make you some toast. You can eat that while we have our tea.' So that's what happened. They ate their tea at the table and I sat there in a chair at the other side of the room and had a bit of toast. I don't want to seem ungrateful – I like a bit of toast as much as anyone – but I didn't really know what to make of all this. I'd not been invited anywhere for tea before, so I didn't know if this was usual or not. I remember sitting there with this slice of toast, thinking, 'Is this weird?'

It's a shame what happened to the Teardrop Explodes, Julian's first band. They were a really interesting group to start with. I had a mate called Gary Dwyer, who was a big bloke and a properly lovely guy. He used to come on the Big in Japan gigs and roadie for us. One day, after rehearsing in Eric's, Budgie had gone home but left his drum kit still set up. I was going to pack it up for him but Gary came over and said, 'I've got an audition for this lads' band as the drummer, but I don't know how to drum. The audition is this evening. Can you show me how to drum a bit?' He'd literally never played the drums before. I was no drummer either, but I got on Budgie's kit and showed him a simple beat that I knew as best I could. It really wasn't great. Then he went for the audition and he got the job. He became the drummer in the Teardrop Explodes. It always makes me laugh when I hear 'Sleeping Gas', their first single, because he's still playing the exact same simple beat from that afternoon and it sounds great.

With the Bunnymen, the whole point was that they were a real band. There were four of them and it was the chemistry between them that made the magic. The Teardrops started like that as well, but then I went to a gig after 'Reward' had been a hit and was surprised to see that everyone except Gary was gone. Julian had replaced them with what seemed like London session men decked out in Spandau Ballet outfits. The strange thing was, no one seemed to notice or say anything. Suddenly there was some bloke with a frilly shirt on and everyone just went with it. I was confused by this. It still seems odd to me that they did that.

The Bunnymen and the early Teardrops were gangs. That's an important factor in the development of a lot of bands. They're young lads, usually, in a room together rehearsing and hanging out. This means that they're together for long periods without other people or the wider world present. They're maybe eighteen, nineteen, twenty years old, and in that world whatever they say is accepted and built upon. When you've got a bunch of mates to back you up, then an echo chamber effect starts and amplifies whatever it is that you're talking about. In that way, gangs start to create their own little universe. Someone like Pete Wylie, for example, always had his gang around him. He could be loud and stupid but his gang was there to back him up. It can be a bit 'the one-eyed man is king' in those situations, but ultimately I still see it as a positive thing. You get all these little worlds forming and they're all distinct with unique personalities. Because of this, a band can have a far stronger identity than a solo artist. It can create a great deal of musical diversity between scenes.

In those days, I think a lot of people in bands felt like they were different types of misfits who became focused, somehow, through their music and their audience and their bandmates. This refined and highlighted their oddness but, at the same time, defined their worlds whereby they found acceptance. This happened through a load of odd or eccentric characters being true to themselves and not compromising to fit in. It's different now. Today, much more effort is made to fit in *in order to* become successful.

People want their own universes reflected back at them, instead of discovering strange new worlds.

Back when I first met Julian and he made me some toast, he must have made a conscious decision to become as weird as he possibly could. It was very much a deliberate choice and fair play to him: he's committed to it. He's still out there, living in a very distinctive Julian-world of his own creation. At the same time that he decided to become as weird as he could, however, I decided that I would hide how weird I was. I was drawn to being invisible. I wanted to play in bands, but I didn't really want to be noticed and I didn't want to be the centre of attention. That's not a great recipe for success in the world I had chosen.

When you look at me during the peak of the Lightning Seeds' success, I've always got sunglasses on and have a beard. You couldn't get a more blatant disguise to hide behind. Part of the reason for my sunglasses was the way you'd always see photos of Phil Spector at the mixing desk wearing sunglasses, so I was probably trying to copy that. But it's odd the way that me wearing sunglasses and Ian McCulloch wearing sunglasses are two very different things. When I put them on, I hide; when Ian puts on sunglasses, he stands out. It makes him look like a star.

I sometimes wonder if my choice to avoid attention was in part because I'm Jewish. I recall growing up with a small but ever-present sense of threat. That can't be the full story, of course, because there are plenty of Jewish people who don't think like me, but at the same time, I do think it was part of it. I'd regularly get comments at school and at Eric's about being Jewish, and the National Front was very big at the time. There were a lot of skinheads about. Not everyone who came to Eric's was on the same side as the Rock Against Racism crowd.

I remember walking home once from Eric's with this skinhead guy who was often handing out National Front leaflets. We were heading across town to a party, and we cut through the grounds where the Anglican cathedral was still being built. It was dark and quite secluded down there at the time. It was about 2 a.m. and we were in a graveyard, and this lad turns to me and he goes, 'You know, Ian, I fucking hate Jews.' I thought, 'Uh oh.' Maybe he had taken me down there to stab me or something. At the same time, I thought I'd better own this, so I said to him, 'I'm a Jew.' He looked at me and said, 'Oh, I didn't mean you. You're all right.' I said, 'How many other Jews do you know?' He said, 'Oh, only you.'

It could get more serious, though. Roger Eagle managed to get Big in Japan booked for a gig in Halifax once. The venue was a big room with a lot of wood on the walls, a really weird place. It looked like an old courtroom. They had a late licence and we weren't due to play until half past eleven, so after we'd done the soundcheck, we had to go off and hang round Halifax all day. I remember we just sat in a nearby pub for hours, killing time, while someone kept putting 'Mull of Kintyre' by Wings on the jukebox again and again and again.

When we got back to the venue, it was crammed full of skinheads. They were all in those shiny green bomber jackets that they used to wear, with the zip pocket in the arms. A crew of Leeds United ultras, who came to this place because they could drink late, they were not the kind of audience who would be impressed by a mad little punk band who only knew five songs.

We started playing to mass indifference at best. We got to the bit in the set where I sang the next song, so I moved to the microphone just as this big skinhead climbed up onto the stage. There was no security or anything like that and someone climbing up on the stage like this never usually ended well. At the gig just before, for example, this big guy had got up, pointed to Jayne Casey and said, 'If she doesn't stop screaming, I'll stab you.' This time, however, the guy comes up to me and says, 'Dedicate this next song to the freedom fighters.' It was not a request.

At this point my mind was racing and I'm thinking, 'Who are the freedom fighters?' I wondered if it was an IRA thing, but the audience didn't look right for that. But the guy was stood there scowling at me, so I did as I was told. I went to the mic and I said, 'This song's dedicated to the freedom fighters.' The crowd roared and to a man they all immediately started *Sieg Heiling*. I tell you, being Jewish in a room full of skinheads performing the Nazi salute is no joke, but when you are stood up on stage and they are all *Sieg Heiling* you, that's a different kind of nightmare altogether.

Around the year 2000, Bill Drummond published a book called *45*, in which he described all the people he remembered from Eric's. When he came to me, he described me as a 'four-eyed yid'. He put it in quotes as if to say those weren't his words, they were just the words that he thought would be the best way to describe me. Those quote marks make you think, 'Who is he quoting? Who was it that talked about me like that?' You want to know but at the same time you don't want to know, in case finding out who it was broke your heart.

The threat. The ever-present threat. It never quite left; it was always there, in the background, and I guess it did shape me to some extent. I still have it to this day. It's not just about being Jewish, I should stress. It's just the way I am. That's what the song 'Permanent Danger' is about on the last Lightning Seeds album – catastrophic worrying that there's always *some* trouble about to reveal itself.

It would be great not to have that feeling and find some way to shake it, but I've never quite managed it. It would be great to be like Julian Cope – fearless, demanding attention. That sense of threat does not go well with the desire to make music for a living. It would be much better to be someone who loved it when all eyes in the room were looking at you. All I can do is acknowledge it and then get up on stage regardless.

27

BOYS CRY

At the point when Big in Japan were thinking of splitting up, in 1978, I was quite friendly with Budgie, our drummer. Neither of us was sure what to do next. I can't remember which of us came up with the idea, but one of us said, 'Well, should we go to London? Should we move there and try to see what happens?' We had no real connections or leads and no real idea what moving to London would entail. Without any thought, we packed a bag, got a ticket to London and got on a train the next day. It was twelve quid for a return saver ticket. We had no plan or any sense of what we were going to do – we had no idea of anything.

By the afternoon of the next day, Budgie and I had arrived in London. I don't know what we were expecting to find. We got off the train at Euston station but we had no idea of where to go or what to do next, but venturing out of the station we chanced upon a poster for a place called the Music Machine in Camden, now Koko. The Clash and the Coventry Automatics were playing that night.

This was the same tour which had come to Eric's a few weeks earlier, back before Big in Japan split. We were still rehearsing in the club in the afternoons back then. When the bands arrived, Bill and Budgie and I would get a fiver each to help load in the gear. That was how we'd met the Clash and the Coventry Automatics a week or two earlier. The Coventry Automatics changed their name later in that tour to the Coventry Specials and then just the Specials. That must have been the first time I bumped into Terry Hall.

So we walked up to Camden from Euston, found the club and hung around the stage door. And as luck would have it, we bumped into Mick Jones from the Clash and the lads from the Coventry Automatics. They remembered us: we were in.

Once inside the gig, I found a couple of guys from Deaf School who I knew. One was Steve Allen, their singer, and the other was Clive Langer, who had briefly been in Big in Japan for a while. Clive was starting to make a name for himself as a producer and he went on to produce bands like Madness, Dexys Midnight Runners, Elvis Costello and loads of others. He was there with the Slits. I don't think he ended up producing them, but he had some connection with them, or else he was working with them in some capacity. Budgie got talking to them in the bar. At the end of the night, he came up to me and he said, 'I've just joined the Slits.' That simple, that quick – I hardly ever saw him again.

After Budgie left, all I had was my bag and my return saver ticket. It was late and I had nowhere to stay. It looked like I was going to be kipping at Euston station and going back to Liverpool the next day with my tail between my legs. Which would have been alright, really. The whole thing about having the idea to move to London and then just going the next day with no plan was that obviously it might come to nothing but you didn't know for sure unless you did it. One thing that you learnt in the Liverpool punk scene was that spontaneous action was more likely to lead somewhere than being cautious and overthinking things.

But as luck would have it, Steve Allen saw that I'd been abandoned. He was living in a squat in Kilburn and he said I could sleep in the spare room for a while. Thanks to Steve, I spent the next couple of years living in London. Decamping to a different city on a whim like that was very different to how it is now, when everyone has mobiles and can be constantly in touch. I remember I phoned my mum to tell her that I was living in London and that I'd be staying there for the foreseeable. She asked me to phone home every three weeks. I said, 'I'm not phoning every three weeks! I'll phone you every six weeks.' I remember thinking, 'God, she's fussing!' Now I'm a parent myself, I see it differently.

While I was in that squat, Steve said, 'Should we write a couple of songs?' That was how Original Mirrors started, although it would turn out to be a wrong turn for me. We got about three songs together and Rob Dickins, who had worked with Deaf School at Warners, very quickly got us a deal with Mercury Records. When it came time to make an album, Rob told us that an American producer called Randy Bishop would be coming over from Los Angeles to produce us. Now, if your name is Randy Bishop, then it's probably not wise to spend time in Britain. But Rob insisted that this guy was great. He said that Randy had come to see him and played him an album he produced and it sounded amazing. I didn't have any say in this, but then I still didn't really know what producing involved or how things were supposed to work – I just assumed that the people who knew what they were doing had it covered.

So Randy flew in from America and we were booked into RAK Studios for six weeks. What was exciting for me was that Rob had booked Phil McDonald as our engineer. Phil was an old Abbey Road engineer who had worked a lot with the Beatles, so it was great to meet him. We started recording and from the off, it was a fraught session. About six or seven days in, Randy fired Phil McDonald, saying that he couldn't work with him and that he had to get his own guy in from America. As he was getting ready to leave, Phil said to me, 'It's been really nice working with you, but that Randy Bishop guy has no idea what he's doing. He is totally clueless. Be careful.'

We waited a few days until Randy's new engineer flew in from America and then we started recording again. It sounded terrible. It wasn't what I had imagined at all. I tried to understand why it was coming out so bad, but Randy just blamed me. He said that maybe they needed to replace me with someone who could play the guitar properly. It was all really upsetting, not least because the tracks sounded so bad. I wondered if I'd ever get the chance to record again after this disaster. It got to the point where I was on the verge of tears. I decided that I'd had enough, so I left and got the train back to Liverpool.

A few days later, Rob phoned me up and listened to my side of the story. He persuaded me to come back to London, where we could all sit down and work out what had gone wrong. Everyone involved met up in Rob's offices for a crisis meeting because all the budget had been spent and I didn't think we had anything usable.

We listened to the tapes and everybody agreed they were terrible. Rob said to Randy, 'I don't understand. You came to my office and played me your stuff. It sounded amazing, it didn't sound like this. Why does this sound so shit?' There was a long pause, then Randy confessed that he hadn't played Rob that album because he'd produced it. He'd played it because he was singing backing vocals on it – he was a session backing singer and that's what he wanted Rob to hear.

Rob had got the wrong end of the stick. Because Randy had flown in from LA to have a meeting with him, he had assumed that he was a producer, not a backing singer. He offered Randy a producing job and, naturally enough, Randy had made the most of the misunderstanding. That's kind of what the music industry was like back then. Mad things like that happened all the time. Everyone was making it up as they went along. I know that I'm probably guilty of romanticising that time, but sometimes when I look at the industry now, I feel like the last gunslinger, staggering out of the desert and finding that the West has been civilised and that the rule of law has arrived. Now, studios are staffed by people with sound engineering qualifications. They have had access to amazing recording software since they were kids. People know what they are doing now. It really didn't used to be like that.

Because the budget had already been blown in RAK Studios, we then had to cobble an album together on the cheap. Back in the Big in Japan days, we'd recorded a demo at a dirt-cheap studio on Fulham Palace Road. This was a tiny little place underneath a used car lot. They recorded the Buzzcocks and the Stranglers there and if I remember right, they'd also done 'Knock on Wood' by Amii Stewart. There was a big guy called Alan who worked there as an engineer. What I loved about him was that whenever the tape machine went wrong, he'd get up from his chair and go over and kick it. It would immediately start working and he would go and sit back down again. He spent his days there, working underneath this car park.

With no budget for a fancy studio, we went and booked into that place. Rob said that I should produce the record because they couldn't pay for anyone else. It might be more accurate to say that nobody really produced it, but that me and Alan got it all recorded between us. I'm not saying that what we recorded was a classic, but it was far better than what Randy Bishop got on tape.

At one point I was working with Original Mirrors in a recording studio in Borough. I never had any money during this time, so I had to pace myself when it came to buying any food. We would rehearse for a few hours, then I'd go out about 3 p.m. when I was really hungry and get something to eat. One day I bought myself a quarter slice of pizza. It wasn't much, but it would have been enough to keep me going until we finished rehearsals. It was a hot sunny day, so I sat outside to enjoy it. Just as I sat down, a car pulled up in front of me, and Iggy Pop got out. He started walking towards where I was. I couldn't believe it. I stood up and I blurted out something like, 'Hi, Iggy!' He looked at me, and then he looked at the slice of pizza in my hand, and said, 'Hey! Pizza! Thanks!', and he took it off me and wolfed it down. Then he walked off. I never saw him again. I guess if you're Iggy Pop, you live in a world where you can just reach out and get pizza whenever you want.

I do have one special memory from my time in Original Mirrors. We toured Europe as support for Roxy Music. One gig was in the Palais des Sports in Paris. Before we went on, I noticed that two ornate chairs had been put by the side of the stage. The implication was that two important people were expected at the gig, but I assumed whoever they were wouldn't bother watching the support band – they'd show up just as Roxy Music hit the stage. We started to play and I looked across and saw that there were two big hairy blokes sat in those special chairs, nodding along. One of them, in particular, looked familiar. It was John Bonham from Led Zeppelin. He saw me looking and he held up his hand and gave me the thumbs-up signal. I can tell you, there is nothing like John Bonham giving you the thumbs-up while you are onstage playing a gig. That was in June 1980 and he was found dead at Jimmy Page's house in Windsor just over three months later, but that one simple gesture of his has lived with me ever since.

28

TALES TOLD

The period after the *Tilt* album, from 1996 to 2006, was a very hard one for me. The Lightning Seeds spluttered to a halt, and it felt like reality hit hard as I emerged from the surreal bubble of a successful and busy period.

The first blow was when my marriage to Becky came to an end. Relationships are a lot about shared experience, which is why I think musicians struggle to keep theirs together. When we got together, we were in Liverpool with all our friends and family and I was producing records locally, so we had a solid homelife. In the early years it worked out okay because Becky could come with me when I was off doing promo. When I was producing an album in Los Angeles, for example, I could bring her with me and our trip to America would be a shared experience. Becky would come to gigs and she would come to the studio.

After *Jollification*, I was no longer a producer in Liverpool. I was in a group, and we were living in London. We had a child, which meant that Becky had to stay at home while I was away, off on tour living the life of the singer in a happening band. In those circumstances, your shared experiences become different. We both found it really difficult. There was no mystery or major drama. I relied so heavily on our relationship but it just seemed to slowly come apart.

It was hard, especially as we hadn't been prepared for what came after. You go from being partners to being co-parents and that's not a relationship status that I think many people are prepared for. Most of us have no models of how that is supposed to work, or good examples to look to. You're pretty much stumbling in the dark as you try to work out what would be best for your child. We've done our best and Becky is still an important part of my life, but Riley was only about eight when we divorced, so our separation was hard on him.

While I was still trying to adjust to all this, my mum died. She was eighty-three and had had mobility issues for much of her life, so it was not a total shock, but losing her still left a big hole in all our lives. Shortly after she died, I got a call from my dad. He said – and this was typical of him – 'I've got good news and bad news. Which do you want?' I said, 'Give me the bad news.' He told me that he had been diagnosed with cancer and that it was fairly late stage and that he wasn't going to have any treatments. I said, 'Why not? Why aren't you getting any treatment?' He said that he just wanted to enjoy his last days as much as he could and that he didn't want to stretch out feeling sick any more than he had to. He said, 'Ian, I'm just going to drink whisky, play golf and borrow money off people that I don't like.' I asked him what the good news was. He said, 'I can't wait to see your mum.'

He went very quickly, less than a year after my mum. Now, I kick myself for the times that I went up to visit him but didn't spend the time with him properly. When I was there, I just needed to escape into town, and I would drink until all hours. I wish more than anything that I hadn't behaved like that and had spent more precious time in his company.

The next thing that happened was that my younger sister Sharon was diagnosed with a brain tumour. She died three months later, in May 2005. She was only forty-four and had three children. Sharon was a social worker in Liverpool and she worked for an agency that cared for young women in trouble. She was a fearless, dynamic and caring person and losing her felt devastating. I could make no sense of it. She was just too young with so much more to do.

Sharon was just a couple of years younger than me, while my two brothers David and Robert were five and ten years older, respectively. Because I was closer in age to her than to my brothers, she was very protective of me. My brother David has a vivid memory of coming into the front room when me and Sharon were little and finding the pair of us fighting. Our parents had gone out and David was supposed to be babysitting. He pulled me off her and had a go at me but as he was telling me to leave her alone, she came up behind him and smashed him over the head with a vase. 'What did you do that for?' he screamed 'I'm trying to help!' She always had my back, even when I didn't quite deserve it – she was pretty fierce, was Sharon.

Losing her after our parents particularly affected my brother Robert. This was my oldest brother, the one who had let me use his spare room to record *Sense* in. He had always suffered from depression, but his anxiety and panic attacks increased. Terry Hall knew a lot about depression and I always found it helpful to talk to him about these things. He was going through a bad patch himself at the time. Then one day he said to me, 'I saw your brother. I bumped into him at Euston station. I don't think he's going to last very long.' I don't know what Robert said to Terry to make him pick up on that, but Terry was right: when he met Robert, he just knew.

Robert's problems increased and my other brother David was constantly occupied with him. He needed almost daily care to function at all, as he was in no fit state to look after himself. His anxiety had got to the stage where he couldn't make decisions or do anything for himself. When you have a family member who suffers from depression or anxiety it's hard because you want to help them. But you can't, not really. There's no magic button you can press. You feel helpless. All you can do is hope that they get better and sometimes that's not enough. Then in October 2006 the phone started to ring: Robert was missing, no one could find him.

Robert had gone to the Anglican cathedral in Liverpool, all the way to the top. It's a massive building. It's the largest cathedral in Britain and dominated by this huge tower, which is well over 300 feet tall. There's nowhere remotely as tall anywhere near it, so you can see for miles up there. He took the lift to the top of this bell tower and waited until all the other visitors and cathedral staff had gone, then he jumped off. He had a note in his pocket, addressed to David. It said, 'This building has no religious significance. It is just the highest building I can find. Sorry.'

On one level, the decision to jump from the cathedral has been hard on those left behind because every time we see the Liverpool skyline, there it is and it brings it all back. But it was in character, in some way. He would want to solve his problems with a grand gesture rather than just slink away. There was something clear and bright about it which was in keeping with who Robert was.

We all take blows in life, but this period was a battering. It was unrelenting. And it all happened over a few short years. All the individual losses piled up on top of each other and it was almost impossible to deal with this cumulative mountain of grief, when you couldn't even tell who you were crying for. I had split with Becky, my parents died, my sister died, my brother died and my career stalled, all in quick succession. It would take me a long time to come back from all that. For well over a decade afterwards I was just dazed. Absent, not myself. It was horrible.

As well as all that, I was also dealing with not having success any more. That's going to sound a bit trite on top of everything that had been going on, and I know it's not the sort of thing that you can expect to receive sympathy for. But the truth is, after you've been so busy and recognisable, it is surprisingly difficult to deal with all that ending. It's not just that it's hard to remember just who you once were, but rather that you never go back to being who you were because you and the world around you have changed. It's an odd sort of limbo. I could see how I'd been knocked off my axis, and separated from my generation. I felt rootless, no longer part of the normal flow of life.

A period of fame affects your sense of who you are and how people treat you. When you meet people, they often act weird. It's very hard to find people you trust. My career had stalled after *Tilt* (1999) and although that was kind of a relief to me in some ways, it put me in a whole new territory that was a difficult place to navigate. After the Lightning Seeds were over – or on hiatus at the very least – I found myself drinking too much. I wasn't looking after myself. I wasn't in a relationship and I was on my own. I didn't know what it was that I should be doing with my days.

I did manage to write and record one album, *Tales Told* (2004), during that period. It's a solo album, rather than a Lightning Seeds record. In some ways, it's not that different from my earlier records, except that I wasn't hiding behind any grand musical arrangements any more. Sometimes after you've taken a beating you don't have the energy or the wit to hide. You just focus on the basics, because that's all you can do.

The songs are stripped back and largely acoustic. On one level I suppose it's not a million miles away from songs like 'Pure' or 'Telling Tales', but I think my songwriting did change around then. It started with a song called 'Blue', which I wrote and recorded just a few days after I split with

Becky. I used this as a B-side for one of the singles from *Tilt*. It was just me singing and playing the piano, so it was much more exposed than anything I'd done before. It wasn't what people wanted from the Lightning Seeds, or so I thought at the time, but it was an indication of what a lot of my songs were going to be like from that point on. Funnily enough, in recent years I've heard from a few Lightning Seeds' fans who say it's their favourite song. Maybe it's aged well and maybe its time has come, but it certainly wasn't anyone's favourite back then. It wasn't what people expected or wanted from me.

The opening track on that album was 'Song for No One'. At the time, there was an American teen drama series called *The O.C.*, which was absolutely massive. It was one of those shows that was a phenomenon for a few years before everyone moves on to the next big thing. They used 'Song for No One' in the opening show of the third series. The entire song was played over a montage sequence of the main characters sailing around the Californian coast in this massive yacht and having heartfelt conversations on an idyllic, empty beach. Now, if any other musician had that sort of exposure, they would have had a massive hit in America. You couldn't wish for a better way to showcase your song. But I just did nothing about it. I should have recognised that a rare opportunity had come my way and got on the phone and taken advantage of it. I just did nothing. Sony never even released the track in America. I don't think they even noticed it had been used on the show.

The photo of me on the cover of the album is probably a good indication of how I felt at the time. I look lost, like I was hungover or hadn't slept. My collar is all twisted and I generally looked uncared for. When I looked at it, though, I saw someone that was still standing. *Just*. That felt like an achievement to me.

29

'WHO THE FUCK IS THAT?!'

In 2013, I was living by myself in a house at the southern end of Portobello Road in west London. I was not doing great, to be honest. I was drinking on my own and sleeping in most mornings. Life had slipped out of focus. Things had become vague and unimportant. I had started to drift.

One winter's day I woke up, hungover, around 3 p.m. It was late November and it was cold and misty, making the world outside my windows look fuzzy and obscured. It looked a lot like how I felt, really. I thought that perhaps I should go for a walk as I didn't really have anything else to do. It was getting dark by the time I made it out of the door. The streets weren't deserted, but they were a lot quieter than they usually are.

I headed up the road, through the mist, towards the market. The streetlights were coming on as I walked. My head was still a mess, but I do remember one thought because it was so clear and sharp: 'I'm so lucky to live here. I'm blessed, really.' A warm feeling kindled in my chest. I looked around and it struck me that Portobello Road was a bit like Mathew Street in Liverpool in some ways, in that they are both magical roads that I had somehow been fortunate to be part of. I wandered over to look at the market stalls. They looked like they were lit by a rich, golden, almost coppery light. Everything was old but beautiful and the items on the stalls were just delightful, piled high with rare, exquisite antiques. Even though I'm not knowledgeable about these sorts of things, I could still see the level of craftsmanship that had gone into making them. My eyes fell on a copper Victorian kettle. The curves of the metal and the warm burnished glow it gave off just stopped me in my tracks. It was such a warm, inviting colour and such a perfect shape that I could do nothing but stare at it. Everything was golden. I had entered a state of Grace.

And then a sudden voice behind me shocked me out of my reverie. 'Who the fuck is that idiot on set?!'

Surprised, I turned. There were a bunch of figures in dark, thick quilted coats over on the other side of the road. I couldn't make out their faces because there were big yellow lights on stands just behind them. The voice then cried out, 'Get that fucking idiot off the set!'

They were filming the movie *Paddington*.

In my dazed state, I had failed to notice a barrier designed to keep members of the public away. I had just walked straight past it, drawn to this golden light, without clocking what was making it or why. A harassed young man and an angry young woman marched up and took me by the elbow. They pulled me out of the light. In an instant, my reverie about this golden magical world and my place in it burst. Instead, I was revealed to be a confused, half-pissed, middle-aged Scouser, in the way and unwanted.

I turned around, went back up the street, closed the door behind me and climbed back into my bed.

30

'DREAMING OF YOU'

The early years of the twenty-first century were for me what I'd call my inbetween days. They were maybe a bit directionless, and not always the most productive. Thankfully, however, they did lead me towards a great positive – my reconnection with Liverpool music via the Coral, the Zutons and my collaboration with the Liverpool label Deltasonic. This gave me the chance to return to my roots, and record and work with these brilliant young Liverpool bands, and the legend that was Alan Wills.

Around the year 2000, I was at a loose end. I was mostly staying home, and not really engaging with the world very enthusiastically. As the song I wrote at the time says, I 'Got No Plans'.

Old schoolmate Nathan McGough came around to visit, and I was telling him how bored and footloose I felt. He mentioned that Alan Wills, another old acquaintance who'd been the drummer in many Liverpool bands, was starting a record label. It was going to be called Deltasonic. He had a tape that Alan had sent him of a band he had found, and Nathan thought it would be right up my street. He played it to me and I was really excited when I heard it. This was the Coral. I listened and I loved it. I thought they were just great and really made me smile. This was at a time when there wasn't much that interested me, musically or other-wise, and smiles were in short supply.

Nathan phoned Alan and told him he was at mine, and that we were listening to the demo and how impressed I was with it. He passed me the phone and I chatted with Alan. 'I love this band,' I told him. 'These guys sound great – make sure you do something with them. Don't let it fizzle away.'

A couple of weeks later, Alan called back. He said that they'd got no money, but did I fancy producing a couple of tracks anyway, just for the love of it? I thought about it and realised that I didn't really have an excuse to say no. I had nothing else to do. Plus the thought that all that potential might come to nothing bothered me. Alan had a reputation for finding and being in bands that were great, but also had a habit of shooting themselves in the foot, then gradually imploding in a haze of weed. I knew that I'd hate it if that happened to this band, and maybe I could help steer a different course. On top of that, it would be an excuse to go back up to Liverpool for a while, which I kind of needed at that point. At this time in my life, it seemed good karma and an exciting prospect. So off to the 'Pool I went.

The band had a rehearsal room on Dale Street, which is just round the corner from Mathew Street and right by the old Cracking Up warehouse. It was a part of town that was a bit desolate, with a lot of homeless people knocking around. I was told to wait for them outside a building on a Sunday night as they were going to come over from the Wirral. I asked how I would recognise them. Alan said, 'Look for a group of about seven lads who look like they're going to mug you – that will be them.' So I got to the building and I was waiting around in the rain at night in the middle of winter. Sure enough, a gang of about seven lads who looked like they were going to rob me turned up. They were really young at that time, and they looked very different that first evening to the image I have of them now.

Niceties dispensed with, they played me a few tracks. Straight away, it was clear they were great. Something special. They were everything I liked in a band – self-formed, from schoolmates who went back years. The bonds between them were genuine and they had a shared worldview and opinions. They were very young with a delicate mix of brilliance and naive ineptitude, which came together in a beautifully compelling blend: they sounded like they were adventurers in their own universe.

I asked them if they had played live much and they said they hadn't. They had done a few gigs a while ago but these hadn't gone well, so they had retreated into a rehearsal room in order to improve. I asked them how long ago these gigs were and they told me it was two years ago. 'Wow,' I thought. 'Had they really locked themselves away from the world and not played to anyone else for two years?' This, though, explained why they had got so good and why they were so fully formed as a band. I'm sure they would have commanded great interest from a label or two, but there was a great affection between the band and Alan, and the dream was a label and independence. Alan pretty much set up Deltasonic for the Coral, and each depended on the other.

Alan was brilliant with young bands and he and the Coral were inseparable at that time. He had found them, he really loved them, and they were very loyal to him. His creativity and enthusiasm were essential for the band to come to fruition. I'm not sure they would ever have left the rehearsal room without his oversight, madcap energy and enthusiasm.

Over the next few years, I got to know them well and became really close friends with them all. I remember going for walks with James Skelly, their singer, along the beach. We would talk about everything, but mainly music and the songs we loved and how we might make some recordings good enough to stand alongside them. He was still really young and living with his grandad, but he was already someone who just lived and breathed music in a way that I could really identify with. He's a sensitive soul with a fantastic work ethic who feels the music really deeply. He is a rare talent, that boy. At that stage in my life, it felt re-energising and inspiring to embrace a new challenge and help the next generation build something special.

It's quite hard to define exactly what my role was in working with the Coral. As I saw it, they needed to be nurtured but not tamed, so there was a job that needed to be done there. Alan had brought me in because presumably they wanted what I had to offer, but at the same time, I wasn't sure exactly what they needed. They didn't require some wise industry elder who they would learn from, as they had such a strong sense of their own identity.

Recording the Coral, then, was quite a combative experience a lot of the time. The first thing I recorded for them wasn't a song that was a favourite of mine, but they insisted we record it. Then we went and recorded their self-titled first record in a rundown studio outside Milton Keynes. They had some great tunes for the album and there were a few songs I felt were key. One of those was 'Dreaming of You' and another was called 'Put the Sun Back'. The problem was that they weren't willing to record either of them.

They were adamant about not including them. It got to the stage where I was almost begging them to record 'Dreaming of You'. It was obvious that this song was the key to their future. I'd seen so many promising bands fail for lack of a good enough single. It seemed terrible that they had such a strong song but refused to record it. They had very fixed opinions, forged in those years of being in a room together with no outside influences. Alan backed them as always, so that song became the focal point of our differences.

Eventually I wore them down. On the final day of the sessions, they agreed to record 'Dreaming of You' on the condition that it would only be used as a B-side. Alan made it clear that he didn't want it on the album and neither did the band. We recorded it pretty quickly, so we still had most of the afternoon left to record 'Put the Sun Back'. Before I could do any more recording, however, I discovered that they had packed their suitcases and ordered a taxi to the train station. They said with a wink that they couldn't do any more recording because Paul had a bad earache and they all needed to head back to Hoylake so he could see a doctor. They picked up their bags and scarpered, looking for all the world like the Bash Street Kids fleeing from some crazy caper.

Fortunately, 'Dreaming of You' was down on tape. Alan listened to it and in the cold light of day, good sense prevailed. It was released as a single and it became their first top-twenty hit and one of their signature tunes. They had finally left their rehearsal room and they were off out into the world fighting the good fight. The album went platinum and I still think they are one of the most important and underrated British bands of the last thirty years. The following year, I produced their second album, *Magic and Medicine* (2003), which became their first number one.

By that point, I felt exhausted. We must have recorded over thirty songs during the sessions for *Magic and Medicine*. Coupled with the combative dramas, I figured that this was a good time to step away and maybe get back to some writing and gigs myself. Then, out of the blue, Alan called. He said that he'd booked Bryn Derwen, a studio in Wales, and that he and the band wanted me to come to Snowdonia and produce the session. I reminded him that, although I loved the band, this was a good moment for me to make some records myself. 'No, you don't understand,' he said. 'They've decided to finally record that song you love,

"Put the Sun Back". They're going to release it as a single at Christmas.' I was thrilled to hear this, and there was no way I could say no. It would be a perfect way to bow out.

I collected my engineer, Jon Gray, and we drove to Snowdonia to join the band in the studio. I told them how made up I was that they'd finally agreed to record the song that I loved so much. But they just looked at me blankly – they had no idea what I was talking about. 'We're doing a Christmas single, aren't we?' I said. '"Put the Sun Back?"' They said they were there to record an experimental mini-album of psychedelic jams called *Nightfreak and the Sons of Becker*.

It gradually sunk in that Alan had just said what he needed to say to get me in the studio. He knew that by the time I'd got all the way to Wales and they had explained the idea, I'd love it and just laugh and get recording. That's pretty much what happened. It still makes me chuckle, thinking about it now. You have to admire Alan for making such a signature Alan move. He visited about a week later, and I told him I couldn't believe that he'd made the whole thing up. He brushed it aside, gave me a hug and said, 'Oh, I knew you'd love it when you got here.'

And he was right: I did love it when I got there. We had loads of fun recording that album. But still . . .

Years later, I finally recorded a version of 'Put the Sun Back'. I thought the end result was brilliant; I loved it. The band, naturally enough, thought otherwise. They didn't release it. They re-recorded it later and released that instead.

There are two bands in my life that I feel a particular affinity with: Echo & the Bunnymen and the Coral. Both are bands that I produced albums for, although that doesn't really begin to get over the impact that they had on me. It didn't end at the studio door. They have remained part of my life ever since. They are my friends and I still feel a very strong connection with – and affection for – both of them. I think of them as family. With the Bunnymen, I'm perhaps a half-brother. With the Coral, I'm probably some weird uncle. But that still counts. That's still family.

31

DON'T FORGET WHO YOU ARE

Producing is an odd business. There isn't really any agreed definition of what the job is and different people see it in different ways. For me, the first step is to fall in love with the band. Some bands you can't love for long, others you never fall out of love with, but I do need to love them when I enter the studio. I have to wish that I was a member of that band and then make the record sound like a distilled version of what I love about them. That's the romantic version I had when I first began working with bands, and I hope it's still a large part of the process now. Beyond that, producing pretty much boils down to knowing what you're doing, and finding out what needs doing, and then doing it. What needs doing is always different for every band.

Sometimes bands are nervous and feeling the pressure, and they are scared of failing. It might be that their last record underperformed and they fear that they are on borrowed time. The label might drop them if the next record isn't a hit. All this stuff is poison to creativity. As a musician, you have to be prepared to fail. You have to be fearless. You have to try stuff and push in odd directions, not knowing if it will work or not. This is true to some extent for live performances as well, but in the studio, it's vital.

Often a big part of a producer's job is helping the band feel comfortable. They need to think of the studio as a safe space to try things which may be amazing, but might also be crap. That atmosphere is something that you as a producer have to get right if a band is to flourish. Bands need to trust you to be on their side. They need to know that you understand and share their vision and that you are there to help them achieve it. Conversely, you're not there to mould them into the record label's vision of who they should be.

Understanding the band's vision is something of an art in itself. One strange thing is that, when you talk to a band and they explain what they are aiming for and what they want to achieve, you realise that how the band see themselves is often very different to how others see them. A lot of the time they even sound different to how they think they sound. Your job then is to understand where this gulf in perceptions comes from. Once you've done that, you can then make them sound how they think they sound. Your job is to basically move them from what they are doing to what they think they are doing.

There's no one way to go about doing this. Sometimes it's as much about what you don't do as what you do. Brian Eno has said that sometimes producing means rewriting the entire song and sometimes it means making the tea. That makes a lot of sense to me. The art, really, is knowing when to make the tea. This means that, after certain projects, you can think that you've done a good job even though it's not always easy to say exactly what you did or how you helped. Sometimes you just need to not get in the way.

The Zutons are a good example of a band where I think my role as producer doesn't quite properly describe what it was that we did, even if I'm hard pushed now to explain exactly what that was. Like Brian Eno, a lot of it was making the tea at the right time, so to speak. I first met Dave McCabe, their frontman, while I was recording with the Coral. He was a mate of theirs. He'd started the Zutons already, but it was early days and they were still a bit unformed. Dave often used to come into the studio when I was with the Coral recording *Magic and Medicine*, their second album. He'd usually pop in during the afternoons. He'd sometimes play me songs that he was writing, and we'd talk about the songs and what was working. I'd then go and watch them rehearse. I was just keeping an eye on them, really, being encouraging and helpful where I could. But at the same time, it was still them who had to make it work. Only they could find the chemistry and personality that would mark them out as special. At that point, it just wasn't quite right. We all felt it. It wasn't quite it, but we didn't know what 'it' was.

Alan Wills had had a role in putting them together. He knew that Russ Pritchard and Sean Payne were good musicians and a great rhythm section. He wondered if they would gel with people like Dave and Boyan Chowdhury, who wrote songs together, and who he saw as a bit of an unpredictable wildcard. The idea was that a solid backing underpinning an unpredictable spark might just work. James Skelly was a big supporter early on, but for a long while Alan wasn't entirely convinced. He worried they would be seen as being too similar to the Coral and he wanted them to develop more of their own identity, which they duly did. The Coral were up and running by this point and they had a real sense of what they wanted to do and where they were going. The Zutons, in contrast, were still finding their feet. Both bands had similar backgrounds and similar influences, but the Coral were the first to distil those influences into a distinct personality of their own. Their self-titled first album was out and selling great, so they were known and the centre of attention. All this tended to overshadow the Zutons.

I remember exactly the moment it all came together. The band had been together as a four-piece for about six months or so and they were playing a gig in Liverpool. Midway through the show, Sean's girlfriend, Abi Harding, got up on stage to play a bit of saxophone. Suddenly, that was the band. That was the missing ingredient that we had been looking for. Abi joined the band full-time and immediately they had it, they were a distinct and fully formed group. It was quite a magical thing to see it happen. I've worked with bands at all different stages of their careers, but no matter what success a band gets or however brilliant they become, there is nothing quite like that initial moment when it clicks into place and all the potential within suddenly becomes visible.

After finishing the Zutons' album, I knew that I was done with producing. Watching the Zutons grow from this early, speculative thing that was looking for its own identity to a fully formed coherent hit band was something that I look back on very fondly. I feel like I was blessed to witness that. I loved the way that, when their album was put out into the world, the world just got it. It wasn't nearly there – it *was* there. I felt like my job was done, in a way. The next stage –

that of managing and maintaining and growing the band in the long term – that wasn't for me. Other people are better than me at doing that sort of thing.

I had been ready to walk away from producing and this seemed the right time. It was around this time that my sister was diagnosed with her brain tumour, so in the years that followed I was in no fit state to give bands the energy and attention that they would need. I've largely kept to my decision not to produce ever since, although I did break it nearly ten years later, when I produced an album for Miles Kane. Miles was the cousin of James and Ian from the Coral, and a songwriter and musician in his own right. He was a different kind of talent – less introspective, and in love with all the attention he could get. This was infectious, and fun to be around.

I had a room in a building in Liverpool called Elevator at the time and Miles was in there, writing songs. We got talking and he asked if I fancied writing a song or two with him. It just happened very easily and naturally. He then said, 'Well, you've written these songs with me, you know how they should sound, how about you come in the studio and produce them?' There didn't seem to be any harm in it, so I agreed. That went well and there was no real drama involved. It turned out to be fun, which is not always the case.

Miles had been to America to record his next solo album, but it hadn't worked out too well and he wasn't happy with the results. Seeing as we'd worked together okay and got good results pretty quickly, he asked if I would be up for writing a few more songs and producing the rest of the album. By that stage, I thought I might as well. If he had asked that from the start, I would have said no, because I'd moved on from doing things like that. Instead, I sort of slipped into doing it bit by bit. It all happened very organically. Miles is such a lovely guy, I couldn't really refuse. It wasn't like we had a business meeting and his people spoke to mine. We just happened to be sitting next to each other and got on.

I feel very lucky to have had that long history with Liverpool music, from Big in Japan to Miles Kane – with Echo & the Bunnymen, the Lightning Seeds, the Zutons and the Coral along the way. So much has changed over those years – not least with the arrival of the internet and the impact of streaming, and the way music has gone from something rare and precious to something constantly available. But I've been around long enough to see what has remained unchanged as well. There is a continuity there. The impulses that drive a musician to make something truly special are the same now as they have ever been. If I had to guess, I would say that even in years to come, with AI music and who knows what else, that will never change.

It will never be easy, but I believe it will always be possible for music to be surprising, thrilling and inspiring. In an unpredictable world, that's a good thing to believe in.

32

FOUR WINDS

I have often been told over the years that the smart move for me would be moving into A&R or having my own record label.

I'm pretty experienced in most sides of making music, from playing live to recording studios, and I'm happy and comfortable working with musicians, managers and record companies, so it would have made sense.

I had my short-lived venture with MCA America around the time of my *Cloudcuckooland* album and later I was briefly an A&R consultant at Sony.

I signed and produced a band called the Rifles. I worked very hard on recording a debut album, *No Love Lost*, and although I was pleased with the results of our creative efforts, I was frustrated by some of the band's decisions.

I had another offer of a label from Universal Records. I thought about which path to take but I reached the decision that I would rather be songwriter and 'troubadour'. It was preferable to me to be playing shows, writing songs and creatively existing in my own universe at my own level, rather than being an executive or label owner.

As far as making music goes, I knew when I was fifteen years old, when I would sit in Calderstones Park in Liverpool on winter days dreaming about songs and music instead of being in school where I was meant to be, that I was in it for life. Music was my obsession, my escape and the place I could go to to dream and get lost in. I was never leaving.

It was an era of great change for musicians and bands, largely due to new technology and the start of the shift in the way people consume music, with more and more people beginning to stream it online. The advances in computing and digital recording had also changed the way people were making records. Traditional recording studios were being used less and less, and big recording budgets became a thing of the past. The days of teenage lads travelling the country in a van from top to bottom to get noticed and toughing out the associated hurdles and sacrifice that went with that lifestyle were replaced by people being empowered by home studios and the relative ease of recording songs to a very high standard that just needed a bit of extra production and a mix.

Schools to teach people about being artists, managers and every aspect of the music business started to change a vocational career into more of an industry you could be trained for. The emergence of social media also really changed how bands were noticed and the way that artists approached things. I would say some things were lost, but there were also great benefits. The future felt very uncertain at that time and I was a little lost at sea, but now that landscape has been defined, I'm a lot more comfortable with it.

Actually, for people like myself, it's been a great positive to be in touch with people through social media and to reconnect with so much of my past career and life. Although these anxieties were running around my subconscious mind, at a time where I was also dealing with the sudden and unexpected losses of my brother and sister, I tried to use my time well and live in the moment, which was something I felt I had struggled to do previously.

It took a while, but gradually I realised that I didn't want a glamorous, carefree lifestyle or a life of parties, drink and drugs. The place I was happiest was in a studio, or on a stage surrounded by guitars, musicians and tape machines. I am a songwriter and producer and that is what makes me happy.

As much as we change over the years, I think the core of who we are remains the same. I can now see why I made the choices I did, like telling Bill Drummond I wanted to take the name Kingbird to avoid becoming a producer, or turning down the opportunity to join my favourite band the Bunnymen. Even then, I knew I had my own story to tell and eventually, at this later stage of my life, I reached the same clarity of thought I always did and decided the way forward for me is simple: you are a songwriter, so go and write some songs.

And so, in 2007, I started recording the album that became *Four Winds*. I had envisaged it as the follow-up to my solo album, *Tales Told*. It was going to have the same openness and simplicity that that album had. Or at least I started working on it with that understanding. But with commercial necessity biting hard, it was decided that it had to be released under the Lightning Seeds name. The thinking was pretty simple – that name would sell more copies than my own name would. Which might have been true, if what I was writing was indeed a Lightning Seeds album. But a Lightning Seeds album that isn't really a Lightning Seeds album was never going to go well.

After it was decided that this *was* the Lightning Seeds, I found myself having to subvert what I was working on in an effort to make it sound less like an Ian Broudie solo album.

It ended up being neither and I felt I had deserted my duty to the songs.

A Lightning Seeds album is, in my mind, essentially positive uplifting bittersweet psychedelic pop, but I wasn't in any fit state to do this at that point in my life. There are a few songs that I still think might have been great if I'd let them be and not tried to force them into a Lightning Seeds setting. 'Four Winds', 'All I Do' and 'I'll be Around' are all songs I really like, but I should have imagined them very differently.

I read a quote from Paul Simon once, after his 1983 album *Hearts and Bones* had disappointed him, where he said that if you don't get the idea clear and the drums and the bass right, then there's no chance of it ever working. I think that's true and I think that's where I went wrong with *Four Winds* – I didn't get the foundations right. As a result of that, it would take me a decade to sufficiently rebuild my confidence to the point where I could make another album.

The last song on that album is called 'I Still Feel the Same'. I wouldn't consider it my finest hour, but I do think that lyric recognises that, although I was in pieces, I did still possess the one thing that would save me and see me through. The song identifies that thing as something I was blessed with when I was little, back before even when I was going to Eric's with all the post-punk kids. That thing was music, or perhaps more specifically, the fact that music was something that I loved. Despite everything I'd been through and despite the doubts I'd had, deep down I still loved it. The last thing I sing in that song and on the album is the line, 'I hope the end for me will live up to the start.' That's a fine hope. The reason I'm able to entertain it is that love of music.

I'm probably simplifying things a bit when I put it in those terms. There were other things in my life that helped to get me through those dark years – particularly Riley, being a dad, and family and friends. We all need community and friendship and support on that level – that goes without saying. But there is something else beyond that. There is something personal as well, some value or drive which lives inside us. This is something that we need, just as much as we need to take care of our relationships and our health and our outer world. After all the loss and the grief of those years, I came close to losing this thing, but ultimately, I didn't. For all that I don't like listening back to that album because it takes me back to those days, I think its very existence does in a way demonstrate that I never lost that precious thing.

33

'SEE YOU IN THE STARS'

At some point I struck up a treasured friendship with Mr Steve Strange – and no, not the Marvel comics Doctor, nor the New Romantic legend. This Steve Strange was the eccentric ex-drummer from Carrickfergus, on the Antrim coast just outside of Belfast, who, against the odds, became one of the biggest agents in the world, working for acts like Coldplay and Eminem and many others.

Steve was like a force of nature – one of those characters that you would run into at various gigs and invariably a couple of hours in his company would lead to some sort of surprising and dramatic adventure that would end late in the night and take a few days to recover from.

He could light up a room with his infectious bellowing laugh and irrepressibly joyous optimism. He knew how to celebrate and nearly always found a reason to, which made him a lot of fun to be around. His party piece was revealing an unexpectedly amazing singing voice and an even more unanticipatedly excellent and theatrical performance of 'Mustang Sally', where he sounded like a cross between Tom Jones, Van Morrison and Axl Rose.

The only thing he loved more than his music and rock 'n' roll were the musicians and artists he represented, and his belief in them knew no bounds.

Our friendship blossomed at a time when I was still at a low ebb, rarely leaving home unless absolutely necessary. Never one to do things by halves, Steve decided to make it his mission to shake me back into action and back to my old self.

One rainy Monday morning, he phoned me to tell me that he was off to LA at the weekend and he wanted me to join him for a week that he had planned that would involve so much fun and be so inspiring that he was convinced that afterwards I would be a new man, re-energised and back in the zone and ready for a new chapter of writing, gigging and recording. I politely declined. 'Ah, but the flights are already booked and can't be cancelled,' Steve said. I politely declined again, but this time he completely ignored me and told me he would be picking me up on the way to the airport on Friday at 11 a.m., and he rang off. So, as it turned out, I really couldn't say no.

He was right, I did have a great time, and I was delighted to reconnect with my old friends John Silva and Danny Benair from my first production trip to LA in the '80s, and to meet some new ones, and I returned ready to start the next chapter of my life and get back to work.

We had many adventures over the next few years, and later, when he was very ill in California receiving treatment, we kept in touch by phone and he continued to book our shows and mastermind our career. Even then, his positivity and enthusiasm were undiminished.

The last time I spoke to him, my phone rang an hour after we finished a jubilant show at the Isle of Wight festival. It was a slightly slurry Steve calling to tell me how proud he was when he had heard the show had been a great success.

He passed away a few days later.

34

'WALK ANOTHER MILE'

My method of writing songs has never really changed. First, you have an idea. Then you find a melody, you find the beat, and you write the words. By this point, you're committed. You have to see it through. You will try to be cool, but fuck cool. You put everything into the recording because in the end, recorded music is the only thing that will last.

The way that I go about this now is by using the Voice Memos app on my phone. When I get an idea for a melody or a chord sequence, I'll play it or hum it into my phone, and chat about what I hope it could be. That way I can come back to it at a later point with fresh ears and see if it's any good.

Working this way forces you to give a name to your songs when you save the file, even though they are still in their embryonic state. These are not the final titles, obviously, but it does help these early ideas take on an identity. It makes them seem like potential songs rather than scraps. For example, the song 'Walk Another Mile' from the last album first shows up in my voice notes under the name 'Q'. This was because one of my first thoughts about it was that it sounded a bit like Q-tip. In truth it sounds nothing like Q-tip, but as that was my first thought, that's what I attached to it. In theory, naming these little ideas helps you find them when you want to go back and work on them some more. But by now, my Voice Memos app has got hundreds and hundreds of little recordings in there, so finding anything tends to be more a question of luck.

As I work to develop these songs further, my phone fills up with new versions of them as I add parts or try things in a different way. Sometimes I'll develop a part and it clicks, becoming a definitive part of the song's final form. Other times, I'll experiment and try something different, but never return to that version of the song. This means that my phone contains blueprints for a whole bunch of alternate directions that the song could have taken but didn't, some of which linger in my mind as much as the chosen final versions, and to some degree haunt me.

The odd thing about these little recordings is that, if I was to play you one before it had been properly worked out and recorded, you wouldn't think much of it. It would sound just like a vague scrap of a thing. It might not even be in tune. You probably wouldn't hold out much hope that it would amount to much. Yet after the song has been finished and recorded and mastered, if you then go back and look at the original scrap, amazingly you can find the whole of the finished song in there. All the character and ideas are suddenly revealed in the original like an oak tree is hidden inside an acorn.

All my songs, from 'Life of Riley' to 'Pure', are about worrying things might disappear. They're about a moment, and the importance of not losing that moment. I always think music's like attack and defence in football. Or like politics. Or like life. It's about balance, and achieving that is the challenge for me. I want to get to the wider world with my music, but not be shit! And getting that is the win. Attack and defence. Make something that will get played on the radio, be a positive thing, and not be shit. That is the hardest thing.

Looking back at the Voice Memos for the album, I can see that from start to finish the album took an embarrassing seven years – and it's not like I was doing a lot else during that time. But I could see how much the world had changed, particularly the music industry, with streaming, TikTok and social media. There's so much talent out there, it can feel intimidating. Where would I fit? Where would I want to fit? *Do* I want to fit? I think the thirteen-year gap between albums was probably in part a crisis of confidence and in part procrastination. But what if I write it and when it comes out, no one notices or cares?

That said, there were other distractions along the way, like 'Three Lions' going back to number one or the twenty-fifth anniversary tour of *Jollification*. That was a really good experience, just because of what it was like to be playing with an excellent band again. It did get a little bit *Spinal Tap* at times, though. I thought we should make an effort with the stage set, so we commissioned a company to build us a giant strawberry. This hung over us, revolving, while we played. It had little lights and mirrors in the pips so that it acted a bit like a giant red mirror ball. I said, 'Oh, it should be about 8 feet tall,' thinking that this would be impressive. You don't realise until you've made one, but an 8-foot strawberry is really extremely large. I used to be terrified when I played that it would fall down and crush us. It needed its own van, driver and dressing room, that strawberry.

I also found the time to play an Ian Broudie career retrospective with the Royal Liverpool Philharmonic Orchestra in 2014, in which I played some Lightning Seeds songs, some from my solo album, and others that I been involved with as producer. It was called One Night in Hope

Street, and was held in the Philharmonic Hall, between two cathedrals and a stone's throw from the haunted flat that I'd lived in many years before. A lot of my friends in bands that I'd worked with were kind enough to join me, and for the songs that I performed by other bands, the original singers joined me. The band consisted of Sean Payne, the drummer of the Zutons, Bill Ryder-Jones and Nick Power of the Coral, my son Riley, and Martyn Campbell, a mainstay of the Lightning Seeds for almost thirty years, a good friend as well as a top-class musician. The guest vocalists were Terry Hall, James Skelly, Ian McCulloch and Miles Kane.

It was a brilliant and chaotic night for many reasons. Years earlier, before I achieved the settled line-up I now have in the band, in some of Riley's initial gigs, the quality of some of the musicians was definitely up and down, to put it politely. Sean had said to Riley, 'I'd love to do a gig with you where you can experience what it is like to play a gig with a great drummer and some amazing musicians. You'd really enjoy it.'

This was the night when Riley got to experience that feeling for the first time. It was an amazing show. Sometimes songs can be overwhelmed by a full orchestra, but that night they felt empowered and supercharged.

The chaotic element came when we realised that somehow Miles had been told the wrong date and was double-booked to play in Dublin that same evening. I was terribly disappointed that Miles couldn't make it to the gig, and typically Steve shared my dismay and couldn't let it happen. I don't think any other agent in the world would care so deeply. Steve decided to pay for a private plane out of his own pocket to fly Miles from John Lennon Airport to Dublin after singing with us, and in time for his gig.

I feel much more confident in front of an audience now with a few years more perspective. I've learnt to trust the songs and I feel as if we are a band in a struggle to excellence, like a football club rebuilding the team to try to climb back up to the Premier League. I'd say we are probably halfway up the Championship at the moment, and we may not get there, if I'm being realistic. But it's all about the journey – it's always the journey that matters in the long run.

It took me a while to get back to that thought, but I made it in the end.

35

THROUGH THE TWISTS AND TURNS

It's difficult sitting here in the summer of 2023, and even harder to believe I'm writing about my friend Terry Hall, knowing that I won't be seeing him this summer, or ever again.

Around this time of year, we would we always be in touch, swapping schedules and figuring out which of each other's gigs we'd be going to over the summer festival season. He'd often travel with us to a couple of shows, and we'd catch up and chat, and maybe make plans to write some songs or go and see a band we were interested in. Every now and again he'd come up on stage and sing a tune or two.

Sometimes I'd just get a message from him saying, 'I see online that you're playing a festival in Tunbridge Wells.

I think I'll come along. When are you going?' You'd tell him that you were getting a particular train from Charing Cross, then you wouldn't hear from him for three weeks. But when you got to the station, he'd be there waiting.

The last time I saw the Specials, they were going to play a hometown gig in the bombed-out Coventry Cathedral. He was quite excited about it in a Terry kind of way, so Riley and I headed up to Coventry. Terry met us at the station. He had decided he wanted to drive us himself to and from the gig. It was a sunny summer afternoon and as we set off into the city, he drove us around a few places that had bittersweet memories for him from his childhood. Then we pulled into the backstage area and parked by the cathedral. It was a fabulous gig – the band and Terry were on brilliant form.

After the gig, we were sitting in the bar and he said, 'I can relax now, because the Lightning Seeds have played. That was the one thing in this entire weekend that I've been most stressed and worried about.' I asked why and he said, 'Because you're really difficult, Ian.' He was hardly the first person to call me difficult, so I reluctantly have to accept there is some truth to this. Terry added, 'Ian, you're one of my best friends. It means the world to me that you're part of this concert.'

Then he said with a cheeky smile: 'But you can be really difficult.'

I've never been criticised so fondly.

I feel as if we were mates for so long that it was pretty much always. I first met Terry when he played Eric's in Liverpool in the late '70s. It was a very early Specials gig if I remember correctly, and they played under the name the Coventry Automatics. Big in Japan used to rehearse in the afternoon in the club before the bands arrived. Roger Eagle would give us a fiver to load the visiting bands' equipment down the stairs and onto the stage. I remember saying 'hi,' but that's about it.

Some years later the Bunnymen were playing Peter Gabriel's festival Womad, and were joined on stage by the Burundi Drummers. I was watching from the side of the stage. It sounded amazing and it was quite a sight. I turned to the guy next to me to say, 'Wow, this is great,' and I realised it was Terry. We chatted more than we had years earlier as we watched the gig, then said 'Ta-ra'.

Not that long afterwards, a lot of the musicians in bands used to have a weekly game of football next to the lake in Sefton Park, one of the beautiful green spaces in Liverpool. It was generally eleven or twelve of us who all knew each other well. I suppose from today's perspective, we made up a very unlikely football team. It was generally Ian McCulloch from the Bunnymen, Michael and John Head from the Pale Fountains, myself, Gary Dwyer from the Teardrop Explodes, and perhaps a couple of Lotus Eaters, and on the odd occasion Pete Wylie of Wah. One day, Gary brought Terry to play. We resumed our conversation, and he asked me if I would like to produce a few tracks for his band the Colourfield. I was thrilled, and agreed straight away. I guess that was the real start of our long-time collaborations and friendship.

A few years later, he called and asked me if I fancied writing a song together. I was about to start recording my second album at my brother's house. We wrote and recorded the song 'Sense'. It was really easy to write together. We had a lot of fun recording it, and he sang backing vocals.

Over the next few years, we worked together often. Terry would come up to stay with me and our families became close. It wasn't that we were 'showbiz friends' or anything like that. He was a proper friend. I don't hit it off with a lot of people on that level very often. I've probably only got a handful of really close friends who have been with me through the years. And all of them are probably crazy.

Terry was writing with a brilliant guitarist called Craig Gannon, who at a very young age had played in Aztec Camera and the Smiths. They asked me to produce an album of songs with them. We recruited Les Pattinson of Echo & the Bunnymen on bass, and my friend Chris Sharrock of the La's, the Lightning Seeds and later Oasis on drums, with the brilliant Cenzo Townshend engineering. We recorded the album *Home* in Liverpool at my studio The Laboratory.

Terry was a master of lyrics and a brilliant vocalist. The chemistry and personalities of everyone involved made it very easy, and it meant that everyone enjoyed themselves. We really laughed a lot and had fun while making the record.

Terry was such a legend and had a hugely successful legacy from the Specials and Fun Boy Three etc., but you'd never have known it from how he acted. Riley and I bumped into Craig recently. He hadn't seen Riley since he was very young, and he reminded us that at that time we lived opposite Strawberry Field next to Calderstones Park. He used to see Riley because Terry, Craig and I would hang out there after we took a break from the studio on sunny days and play some tennis in the park. Riley said, 'I don't remember that. Wow, I really can't imagine Terry playing tennis.' Craig laughed and said, 'No, he didn't – me and your dad did. Terry was ball boy!' That beautiful and hilarious memory suddenly popped back in my head, and it made me really smile, because that was the Terry we knew.

Thinking back, there were many different sides to Terry over the years. He went through changes, but he'd always surprise and inspire you creatively and emotionally. There was no one more generous. After the Lightning Seeds' third album *Jollification*, I had agreed to play live gigs, but I was extremely nervous at the prospect of live vocals. He suggested that we play four or five gigs together. 'If we use more or less the same band,' he said, 'and you just see your mate singing, and then you sing a bit, that's bound to make it easier.' We did the shows like that, and it did get me onstage. It was such a kind and thoughtful gesture.

I think I was always a bit in awe of Terry. He was so natural onstage in a way that was quite understated but full of charm, and always cool. He never seemed to be putting on a front, or trying to impress. He looked like he was born to be there. It's a rare quality that I would have loved to have had. We were quite different characters in a lot of ways, but that was never any problem. Being a musician in a band is a uniquely odd situation and to some degree we shared a lot of issues related to that. When I had tough situations that probably hardly anyone in the world would understand, I knew that I could always tell him and he would get it straight away. He would know what to do. Terry was always there for me – he was solid, and I hope I was for him, too.

As I've said, I always had the feeling that I was looking for the right singer, and that the only reason I became a vocalist was because my singer never showed up. I've always felt that I just needed the right musical band mate – a Mick to my Keith, or a Mac to my Will, but I just never found that person. And really, looking back, I think that person was

Terry. We would have been great band mates, and it would have been a great band. We talked about it a few times over the years. Ultimately, though, we both always had too much going on separately to find the time to make a record together as a group.

Tragically, Terry became unwell very suddenly, and then very unwell very quickly. One minute we were in a fairy-tale setting in Somerset at Riley's wedding, with Terry and his wife and soulmate Lindy. Then, in just a few months, he was gone. It was truly devastating.

I said a few words at Terry's funeral. In my eulogy I quoted two lines that resonated strongly with me from his lyrics to a Lightning Seeds song called 'Like You Do', which we wrote together. I chose those words because they seemed to sum up how Terry lived his life. He could always see clearly what was important. He knew who mattered and what didn't. He knew who to celebrate. Those lyrics he wrote are: 'Be everything you are and cherish what is true / Celebrate the ones who need to be with you.'

Terry had a unique aura. He was a guide through treacherous waters. He was a star – inspirational, enigmatic and charismatic. He was my friend, and I really miss him.

36

FOOTBALL AT CHRISTMAS?!

It's a strange and wondrous thing when a song connects with something in the human psyche, in a way that elevates it to a place where different rules apply. Some songs just achieve that instantly, whilst for others it takes years. It can happen because of a movie, or an artist becoming legendary. And then some songs just take on a life of their own for no tangible reason at all. These songs can go worldwide, crossing cultural boundaries and generations.

During all these years, 'Three Lions' has never gone away. There were times when I would think that it was fading from people's memories, but it would always come roaring back. It's a mixed but amazing and humbling feeling to hear a stadium sing a song that you created, and I wish I'd written more of them.

In the years immediately after 'Three Lions' became an anthem, everything flipped. Prior to that, no one in an indie band thought about recording a football song. Not even me, really. For a few years after, though, it seemed that everyone wanted to do one. There used to be all these stories in the papers about how the FA were deciding between massive artists who would all be scrambling to make the next one. People like Robbie Williams, Ant & Dec or the Spice Girls would be vying to get the gig. It was a crazy time, but I guess the thinking was that doing a football song was an easy way to have a big hit, and we were treated to quite a few of them.

In 1998, we agonised over whether to make a new version of the song for the World Cup. In the end, for better or worse, the temptation was too much to resist. 'Three Lions 98' was born, but this time the FA were not on board, and it was unofficial. We knew that the original version, which was emotionally tied into a pretty successful tournament for England and memories of that golden summer, would be a hard act to follow. Yet it did really well, and topped the charts. We had fun making a video and generally promoting it, but I thought that was probably the end of the story.

For the next twenty years or so, we resisted revisiting it and left it to its own devices. As the years went by, affection for the song grew. It seemed to take on a new identity, and it would resurface with every glimmer of hope when the team played well.

In 2018 – with the World Cup in Russia, and another glorious summer coupled with a strong performance by the team – a new generation seemed to discover the song. The world had changed with the advent of streaming and social media, and every day there seemed to be another meme of movies with 'Three Lions' added in. Then there were performances of the song by everyone from school classes to the royal guardsmen choirs or people in railway stations – anyone who felt like it really. Some of them were hilarious, and some were moving. It was brilliant, and I enjoyed it every bit as much as when we had made the original release. It felt like the song was firmly embedded in the country. It became everybody's song. That changed how I thought of it, and actually made me much more comfortable performing it live. Then of course as soon as England lost, it dropped from number one to number ninety-seven in the charts. According to the Official Chart Company, that became the new record for the fastest – and longest – drop from the number-one spot.

The Qatar 2022 World Cup was held in December, the temperatures there in summer being just too hot to play football in. This made it the only World Cup that would be held around Christmas. The idea of doing a Christmas version of the song, then, was something that we couldn't help but think about. We couldn't decide whether doing that would be genius or terrible. As Frank put it, football songs are naff and Christmas songs are naff. But in physics, two negatives make a positive, so it might be so naff that it transformed into something glorious.

There were problems with the idea, though. Although the final was the week before Christmas, most of the games in the Qatar World Cup were in late November or early December. If England were to have a Christmassy World Cup, they would need to make it through to at least the quarter-finals. We'd already seen how the last number one plummeted when England were knocked out, so we knew how much the success of the song would be tied to how the team did, and that was out of our hands. It's a song of hope and belief, so naturally people only really want to hear it if they are hopeful and they believe.

Then the Women's Euro 22 kicked off. That competition had everything I love about the game, but without any of football's dark side. It had none of the hooliganism, the xenophobia or the obscene amounts of money that ruin the men's game. It was a pure joy, really, and because it was held in England, the whole country got interested in a way that we hadn't seen before. The phrase 'It's coming home' was in the air again. The idea that only the men's game was important and that the women's game was somehow lesser – that suddenly seemed weirdly old-fashioned and stupid. The skill and confidence of the women's England team changed all those attitudes. By the time they were due to face Germany in the final, the whole country was hooked. Normally when England face Germany, we have this sense of dread. We think that we're going to be kicked out, probably on penalties. That's the legacy of the Euro 96 semi-final defeat right there. But there was something about the women's team that made you think that things could be different.

Watching the press conference after they had won the final was such an amazing moment – surprising, joyous and thrilling. I was so excited to be a little part of it. The head coach Sarina Wiegman was seated behind this desk in what looked like a lecture theatre, with the world's press in front of her and the board with all the sponsors' logos behind her. It was unfolding like a typical post-match press conference, when you started to hear voices singing, 'It's coming home, it's coming home . . .' from outside the room. Then the whole of the England women's team, still in their kits, burst in singing. They danced around the desk and climbed onto it, punching the air. It was a moment of impulsive, unfettered joy. Then they all cleared off again.

For me, it just felt like the song had taken on a new level of meaning. 'It's coming home' was a reference to the last competition to be held in England in 1996, so of course it should also be applied to the next competition to be held in England. And in the women's Euro 22, we finally won. Our hopes and dreams had finally come true. That it was the women and not the men who got to bring the trophy home seemed fitting, in a way. It seemed to emphasise a change in British culture as we have moved from the twentieth century to the twenty-first. Absolutely it was their song now, and I guess from the perspective of history it was always fated to be.

In response, we did a new version of it that summer, at a gig at the Electric Ballroom in Camden. We rewrote the lyrics to be about the current Lionesses squad and had a bunch of retired Lionesses – Faye White, Rachel Brown, Anita Asante, Fara Williams and Rachel Yankey – on stage doing the backing vocals to help remind people of the history of the women's game. In many ways it should have been the perfect end to that song. We'd dreamt that England would win the Euros and take the trophy when they were hosted at home, and twenty-six years later, that's exactly what happened. It felt like the song had held that dream and kept it alive over all those years. Now the Lionesses had made that dream reality.

The problem was that we enjoyed that gig and the Lionesses' summer so much. The knowledge of the December World Cup hung tantalisingly just in front of us, and we couldn't resist.

It was always going to be a gamble. It was a funny World Cup in all sorts of ways and there were a lot of reasons not to embrace it fully. We'd all read the endless press coverage of the corruption at FIFA and the question marks about why Qatar had been chosen to host it. Then there was the issue of human rights and the conditions of the migrant workers. Frank and David rewrote the lyrics for the third time and it was tricky to know the extent to which this should be addressed. Our feeling was that the game of football itself was a separate thing to the goings-on at FIFA and that all their corruption shouldn't be allowed to taint it.

The new version of the song – now called 'Three Lions (It's Coming Home for Christmas)' – began with the song being sung by the Lionesses as they gate-crashed Sarina Wiegman's press conference. The video had Geoff Hurst in it – *again* – this time dressed as Santa, along with Bethany England and Jess Carter. We had no idea what people were going to make of it.

I had a surreal moment when I saw an edit of the video. This put me, Frank and David as we are now into the 1996 kitchen scene set, alongside the versions of us as we were back when we filmed the original – the idea being that it would illustrate how long we've held on to the dream and how football is a constant in your life. When I was watching the finished video, a shot of me making the tea appeared, and my mind went, 'Oh, here I am.' Then this old bloke entered the shot. I thought, 'Who the fuck's . . . Oh no! Actually, that's me!' I guess we all see ourselves differently in our mind's eye. I still see myself as the younger guy in the frame. Most people are spared such a blatant image of their own mortality!

The video seemed to hit a nerve and went viral, and it reached a million views on YouTube in its first twenty-four hours. But the country hadn't really embraced the competition as they usually did, partly because of doubts about holding it in Qatar, and partly, I guess, because of a feeling that England weren't quite where they needed to be. This doubt solidified after their second game, when they drew 0–0 against the United States. England made it through the group stages okay, and then beat Senegal 3–0 in the round of sixteen. You could feel glimmers of hope starting at that point, but it was all very cautious. Everything hinged on the quarter-final game against France. The country didn't really feel like it had in the previous summer tournament, with people flying flags from cars and pub gardens full of fans. It felt like if we won the France game, people were ready to become fully emotionally invested in the tournament, and our record. But, alas, it wasn't to be.

On the song 'Great to Be Alive', from the last album, the first lyrics I sing are: 'Hope lives in young men's hearts, it's the key to their charm, it keeps them from harm.' I suppose I was thinking that we lose that willingness to have a go as we get older. In a way, I'd say that hope was at the heart of 'Three Lions', and that's a terrible thing to lose. So, in that spirit, I'd say that the Christmas version of the song could have gone better – but I'm still glad we did it.

'Three Lions', I know, is what I'll be remembered for. It's the headline. Its shadow obscures lots of other things I'm very proud of, and that's a bit of a shame, but I'm proud of it and glad to have it in my life. There are songs that become so well known that no one thinks of them as things that someone once wrote. With songs like 'Happy Birthday' or the National Anthem, they just exist and they feel like they've always existed. Everybody knows them, but if you asked anyone who wrote them they'd have to go on Wikipedia and look them up. They are songs that have outgrown their songwriters.

I'd love 'Three Lions' to become that.

37

BOUND IN A NUTSHELL

At a certain point, writing and releasing songs felt a little pointless. People I had loved had died, and it felt overwhelmingly like there was more to life than sitting in a studio worrying about melodies. I felt that I had made an error in perhaps prioritising my music over my life. I ground to a halt creatively and searched for something else. But in the end, everything led back to music. I started writing songs again and tentatively playing some shows, and then, aided by Steve Strange and Riley, the Lightning Seeds has become gradually reborn.

I love my band, I love playing live shows, and I even love 'Three Lions'.

Earlier in my life, making records was a much more sociable affair. Everyone gathered in the studio, drank tea, maybe ate toast, and spent the day chatting and recording and generally having fun making records. Nowadays it's a lot more solitary. It's still fun, but a lot of time is spent in front of a computer, and the time you get to spend with other people is limited to when you are playing shows, rehearsing and travelling. I think it's probably no coincidence that this is now my favourite part of being in a band, and where I want to be.

Terry and Steve's deaths reinforced that feeling for me, and they have had the opposite effect to my earlier losses. After Terry had gone, the incredible outpouring of affection for the work he had left behind seemed undeniably precious and valuable. A life making music now feels to me one well spent. I recently bought a warehouse in Liverpool to use as a base where I can record, rehearse and generally hang out and be creative.

Riley has become my manager now, which has also helped to invigorate me. It's a job he's great at because he's always been more sensible than me. I remember when he was about seven or eight years old and he used to stay with me most weekends. We would play tennis and watch football, but what he really loved was to watch the Beatles Anthology videos. We were both enthralled by them.

At the time the amazing Zak Starkey – Ringo's son – was drumming for us. He called to invite us both to a fete near his dad's farm, where Ringo and various noted musicians might get up and play a few songs spontaneously in a very relaxed environment. It sounded great and we were excited to attend. We had a lovely afternoon and after a while Zak came over and asked Riley if he wanted to say hi to his dad. I felt Riley grip my hand very tightly and back away.

'No thanks,' he said.

I was amazed by this. I said, 'But you love the Beatles, and especially Ringo. Are you sure you don't want to say hello?'

Riley was adamant that he didn't, so Zak didn't push it and left us alone. Riley looked relieved and I asked him again what the matter was. He whispered to me, 'In the video, Ringo said he takes drugs and I think he might be dangerous!'

We had just watched the episode where Ringo and Paul were talking frankly about LSD and the Swinging Sixties, and I had noticed that he seemed a little confused and unsettled by it. He was at the point in his school education when the evils of drugs, drink and cigarettes were being drilled into him, and his teachers had told him that he must stay away from anyone who used them. They certainly did a good job convincing him, and he took the warnings very seriously.

I laughed and I wanted to explain that Ringo wasn't what his teacher had in mind, and that I was sure he'd be very safe with him. I bit my tongue, however, as this wasn't an easy conversation to have with your eight-year-old. Fortunately, he did get the chance to meet Ringo some years later. He was a teenager by then, and his views had definitely mellowed.

I'm uncertain of the next chapter, but I'm looking forward to a lot of time next to the Mersey in my studio, surrounded by friends and music. It's in a slightly forgotten area of the city centre, but it's an area I remember fondly. This was the place where my grandfather and my father worked, which I would often visit as a child back in the 1960s.

My family's links to this area are down to my paternal grandad, Louis Broudie. Around the year 1900 or so, he lived in a little village somewhere between Riga in Latvia and the Russian border. When he was about fourteen, Cossacks would raid the village and kill the young men. My grandad and his two brothers decided that they had to get away. They fled from their homes and lost touch with each other, but before they became separated, they agreed that if anything happened, they would all head to New York and try to meet there.

So my grandfather crossed Europe on his own and managed to get passage on a steamer to the US.

Eventually his ship docked and the ship's crew told him that he had arrived in New York. Coming from the Latvian countryside, he had never seen a city as big as this before. He looked out at this strange city with huge, tall buildings and people speaking English in a strange accent and he got off the boat and wandered around awestruck, wondering how he was ever going to find his brothers in a city of that size. He only spoke Russian, and he knew nobody there. Eventually he managed to settle, and it was then that he was dismayed to discover that he wasn't in New York after all: he was in Liverpool. The staff on the ship had lied to him to get him off the boat, so that they could sell his berth again. Apparently, that used to happen quite a lot.

My grandfather settled in Liverpool and opened a tailor's shop not far from Lime Street station. He got married and had a family and made a good life for himself. This random series of events is the reason that, first my father, and then myself, were born in Liverpool.

Decades passed, but he never gave up on the dream of finding his brothers again. In the '60s, he used to make uniforms for sailors who came in from the docks, and one day an American guy came in and my grandad measured him up for a new uniform. The American noted my grandad's name and asked if he was any relation to the Broudies of Texas, whom he knew back home. My grandad said he didn't know, but told him his story and how he still hoped to one day find his brothers. He gave this American sailor a letter to take back with him and pass on to the Texas Broudies.

Some months after this, a letter with an American postmark arrived at his tailor shop. It was from his brother, who had settled in Texas. My grandad was ecstatic. After all these years, he had found one of his brothers! He was just so thrilled. They wrote to each other, and his brother made plans to come to Liverpool to visit him. But when my grandad fell ill, my family wired his brother in America to tell him that he was very sick and that if he wanted to see him, he would have to come immediately. He set off at once, but unfortunately he arrived two days after he died. The brothers who left that village in Latvia all those years earlier never got to see each other again in this life.

As his grandson, I'm so glad he got off that boat on the Mersey River and made his life here in Liverpool. There's really nowhere I would rather be from . . . not even New York.

38

'YOU'LL NEVER WALK ALONE (REPRISE)'

On Saturday mornings when I was a little kid, my uncle and some friends would come over to our house. We'd all have dinner together, then they'd cram into a car with my dad and sometimes my older brothers, and they'd go off to Anfield to watch the match. I'd watch them drive away, desperate to go with them. I longed to be able to see Liverpool play in real life. There wasn't much football on the telly back then, and what there was didn't seem as exciting as going to a game and seeing my heroes. For the longest time, I was told I was too little to go with them.

Then one wonderful day it was decided that I was probably old enough. This was September 1964, and I was six years old. I was told that I could go with my dad and my uncle to a midweek evening game, which was Liverpool v. Leeds. I was just so excited, but still totally unprepared for what it would be like when I walked into the stadium. It hit me hard, and it was something I'll never forget.

The floodlights were a big part of it. They made everything appear so bright, the colours so intense. I'd never seen grass as green as that pitch before. When the players came out, the Leeds kit looked whiter than any white I had ever seen; they were shining. When Liverpool came out in bright red, they looked how heroes are supposed to look. The only professional football that I had seen before was on TV in black and white, and TV screens were tiny in those days, so I suppose that was all a part of why I found the real thing so overwhelming. Normal life had never been this vivid.

I remember we had seats and the Kop was on our right, so we must have been in the main stand. In those days, everyone used to talk to each other at the game. People would pass round cigarettes to whoever was around them. I'd never seen my dad and my uncle behaving like that before. This was a part of their lives that I was seeing for the first time. I could see how happy they were, just being there.

But what really got me was the singing. I'd never heard my family sing before. I don't know if I'd ever even seen grown-ups sing, come to that, let alone 50,000 of them. And what a glorious sound it was. When it started up,

I just looked around, thinking, 'What's going on?' The terrace hymn was 'You'll Never Walk Alone', which would have been a new thing back then as Gerry and the Pacemakers' single had only come out the year before. But it was as if it had already become a longstanding tradition. Now of course it's the club's anthem and those words are on the club's coat of arms and above the Shankly Gates, so maybe that *has* coloured my memory. 'You'll Never Walk Alone' is not one of those triumphant songs about being the best or beating others. It's a song about community and how that supports us all. It was there at Anfield, when I was six years old, that I learnt what a football song should be.

Also, in my memory, everyone was singing Beatles songs. I think that's true, but I've seen footage of '60s Anfield crowds singing 'She Loves You', so I can't be sure that that hasn't coloured my memories. But I suspect I do remember it right, because that night was just such an overwhelming experience. Everything about it was burnt into me. We came from behind and won 2–1, as well.

What I discovered that night was that music, emotion and football could come together and be fused into one experience. At the heart of that experience was togetherness and family. When that happened, it was just great – a brilliant, brilliant thing, as good as it gets. I think I was very lucky to experience that at such a young age. I'm a fair bit older now but it seems to me that what I learnt that day is still true. That is what life is all about, surely? I'd be hard pushed to think of anything better.

Shortly after going to Anfield, I was taken on another, potentially life-shaping trip to see the Beatles in concert at the Liverpool Empire. This was my first gig and I was still only six or seven. My older brothers had got tickets, but my dad would only let them go if they took me as well. He knew how much I loved the Beatles. My brothers didn't want to take me because I was so young, but they had no choice.

We got to the Empire and we were engulfed by a crowd of thousands of hysterical screaming girls. It was the most terrifying thing I'd ever seen. Why were all these older girls losing it like that? I had no idea. They were so loud, it was unreal. The noise that those girls were making seemed louder and more dangerous than even the noise of the crowds at Anfield. There was something feral about it all, a madness in the air. I was frightened and started crying.

My brothers didn't want to take me out of the theatre because then they'd miss the Beatles. They said to me, 'Sit down in your chair, put your fingers in your ears and close your eyes.' So that's what I did. I sat there crying with my fingers in my ears throughout the whole thing.

When you tell people nowadays that you went to see the Beatles, they often look astounded. It's as if you were present at one of the great moments of history – but while I did go to a Beatles concert, I didn't actually hear them and I didn't actually see them. For me, the whole experience was nothing but terror.

Again, my trip to see the Beatles is one of those stories that seems almost too prophetic. I was drawn there by my love of music. That music was all that I wanted and, to my mind, all that mattered. But the reality of Beatlemania meant that the music was drowned out by everything peripheral. The fan worship and adoration got in the way and turned something positive into a nightmare. It meant that I could not hear what I went there to hear.

Years later, when I was going to Eric's, we were all fans of the bands that played in the club. We used to love people like the Fall and Joy Division and we would argue about the merits of all the acts for hours. But when the bands got off stage, they would just hang out in the club with us. You could chat to them, or you could leave them alone, it didn't matter. They were people we could relate to. There were often more outlandish and glamorous people in the audience than there were on stage. We all worshipped the music, but we didn't really worship the musicians that made it. Instead, they inspired us. We thought, if they could do it, then there was no reason why we couldn't do it as well and maybe even do it better. That to me seems to be what musicians are there for. We work hard at our music and if we lift ourselves up by doing that, that should potentially lift the audience up with us as well. The out-of-control screaming at the Beatles concert was the opposite of that, or so it seemed to me. It worked against the music. I was not, clearly, cut out to be a pop star. You can see how the world of '90s Britpop celebrity would be a difficult place for me to inhabit.

After my parents died, my brother found this Super-8 film footage of us all as kids. It was a bit of a surprise as we didn't know that anything like that existed. Being a middle child, there's not a huge amount of photos of me as a kid. The footage of me is so on the nose, it's almost spooky. There are only two short clips of me. They were both probably taken around 1964, around the time I went to my first match. In the first clip, I'm jumping up and down on my bed, holding the first Beatles album over my head. The Beatles were my first musical love and they'll probably be my last. I was born in Penny Lane, which is a fact that still makes me happy. We lived in Menlove Gardens, which was down the road from John Lennon's house in Menlove Avenue, just past Strawberry Field, so the Beatles loomed really large in my childhood. Their world was my world, or at least that's what it felt like.

In the second clip, I'm in the garden with a football and I'm jumping over it. That's the only two little clips of my childhood that exist, one of me celebrating music and one of me playing football. It's my life in a nutshell – it's as if everything that happened was fated from that moment on. In those clips, I'm like one of those little scraps of song ideas that I have on my phone, which are unfinished and rough but still contain the heart and spirit of what they will eventually grow into. Looking at those clips now, I'm struck by how happy we all look. We're all playing or tickling each other or giggling. I thought I was more of a moody or sensitive kid, but in those surviving clips, I'm just beaming.

I didn't know at the time just how lucky I was, really. Music and football, the things that I cared about most as a kid, were in the midst of their glory years – in our city at least. Liverpool were league champions and we were about to win the FA Cup for the first time. On top of that, the whole city was buzzing about the success of the Beatles. We were very proud of how well our boys were doing. Everything seemed up. Many people aren't lucky enough to experience anything close to that. Liverpool in the mid-'60s was a perfect time for a six-year-old kid to get their first record and go to their first match.

Maybe this is part of the reason why I'm often reaching for something bright and positive with the Lightning Seeds. When you have had a taste of things that are golden, you never forget it. You always know it is how things are supposed to be – to aim for something less just seems ridiculous.

39

'FIT FOR PURPOSE'

One of the advantages of having two brothers who were a good bit older than me was that I got to hear their music from a very early age. All I had to do was sit out on the landing when they had their friends over and the records came out. Because there were five years between them, you would hear different types of music depending on whose door you sat outside. With my older brother Robert, it would tend to be the Beatles, Dylan or folk artists like John B. Sebastian and the Loving Spoonful. David was five years younger, so the music I heard through his door tended to be heavier and more electric – things like Cream and Jefferson Starship, along with blues or more progressive stuff. His mates all had long hair and they were always in my brother's bedroom, smoking weed and jamming along on their guitars. My mum was not happy. She would always shout, 'The house stinks of cannabis, open the windows!' That became the standard line whenever they were gathered in there – 'What's that smell? Open the windows!'

I phoned David the other day. He picked up and said, 'Hang on a second, Ian, I'm just jamming to a record.' He had his amp set up and he was playing lead guitar all over a bluesy jazz record that he had on. He's seventy now, my brother. 'Do you still do that?' I asked, and he said that he did, all the time. 'Wow, how lovely,' I thought.

Later on, when I was twelve or thirteen, I was given a guitar of my own. It came from Woolworths. It was an Audition electric guitar that came with an Audition amp and I think it cost £24. Belinda Stone, who later married John Power from Cast, used to live with her mum and dad across the back garden. She once said to me, 'My dad used to hate you. All he could hear was electric guitar all day, it used to disturb the whole road.' People in the street used to say, 'Ian's playing his bloody guitar again.' I used to play 'For Your Love' by the Yardbirds over and over, singing all of the words, not knowing any of the chords. At some point one of my brother's friends drew a little diagram of three chords for me, but that was the closest thing I ever had to a lesson. I was a self-taught guitarist playing along to records and probably getting it all wrong. I still think there is value in not getting things quite right. Those are often the moments when something unanticipated can happen and bring a song to another level.

Around that time, I got a record player of my own in my room. I had a pair of Wharfedale Linton speakers and a TEAC deck. The turntable wasn't earthed properly. This meant that if I went to lift the arm off the record at the same time that my other hand was touching the strings on the guitar, I would get a massive electric shock. I would be thrown backwards and a fuse would blow, cutting all of the power in the house. That added a layer of jeopardy to the whole thing. Maybe that's what forced me to learn fast and to get it right.

I used to get stoned, put a record on and sit in front of those speakers for hours. Each song I played was like a world that surrounded me. The world of sound was so much more interesting than the normal world. This was the world I always wanted to be in, there was always a little more to explore. Every time I visited, I'd discover something new. In front of those speakers, I'd see how the instruments sat next to each other, or combined with each other, or clashed. I saw how all the different elements had space and prominence, how much they contributed to the bigger picture. I saw the structure of songs and recognised when repeating parts worked and when the song needed something new. I saw when parts were missing and I saw when there was too much. I saw how melodies affected me and rhythm too. The real world could be confusing and difficult, but the world of music was something that I could understand. As I turned up the sound, I dialled down the regular world.

The strange thing about this world of sound was that it was something that people had made. You could see the joins; you could see where the decisions had been made about how it should sound and how it was put together. A lot of the time, a record would annoy me. The way it had been made wasn't right. The music as recorded wasn't what the song wanted to be. It seemed unbelievable that people had released the record that way.

I used to sit there, lost in the fantasy of taking the music apart and putting it back together in a different way. After the record finished playing, I'd be thinking about it for ages. To me, it just seemed a terrible shame that the song wasn't perfect because it should have been; it deserved to be.

So I sat there, hour after hour, day after day, listening. I wasn't great in school, but this was something I could do: I could listen. I never considered any job or career outside of music, even though I didn't know what a record producer was, back then. But I knew that people could write songs and be in a band because I knew that Lennon and McCartney did that, and they were from where I lived, so that seemed real. Achievable, even. I always knew that music was something that I could make.

When I had headphones on, my mum and dad downstairs would hear me rocking in my chair while I listened to music. They started to get worried about me. I was so intensely focused on listening to records that I would just sit there, rocking backwards and forwards. They thought that when I was like that, they couldn't quite reach me. They'd beg me to take a break every now and then – they thought there was something wrong with me.

Maybe because she was concerned about my mental health, my mum often made a point of telling me that I was physically in full working order. I never used to think of my mum as being disabled, but I guess that's what she was. She caught polio as a child and although she recovered, her leg was never the same again: she wasn't able to bend it at the knee. Her response to this was to just ignore it and carry on as if everything was normal. There were things that her leg stopped her from doing, such as driving a car (she wasn't able to put her foot down on the clutch). But in general, she didn't let it define her or hold her back. She would probably be annoyed with me for describing her as disabled, even though when she was old, she and my dad did begrudgingly get a disabled badge for the car. She may have been physically limited, but she had great courage and determination.

Although she didn't let her leg hold her back, she still took great pride in me and my brothers and sister being physically able. When I was a kid, I remember her telling me, 'Look at you –you can be anything you like. You're fit for purpose!' As she saw it, I had no excuses. I may have been rocking in a chair for hours, but I had a fully working body and there was nothing holding me back. She wanted me to know that there was nothing I couldn't do. I probably didn't quite understand where this was coming from at the time, but she instilled in me the feeling that someone believed in me, and that you could aim high and live the life you wanted, with no limitations or boundaries that weren't self-imposed. That's a great thing to hear as a child. Her words became the song 'Fit for Purpose' on the last Lightning Seeds album.

My mum's words might explain why I've always had a single-minded belief that I would be a musician. At that time, a lot of people from backgrounds like mine didn't see a way for themselves to work in the arts. Because they don't grow up around people who do things like that, it can feel like it's an irresponsible pipe dream, and that it is wrong for you to even entertain the idea. I was actively discouraged at school. But I never had any of those doubts – I don't think my mum ever doubted I could do it either.

Back when I was a little boy sitting out on the landing, listening to music drifting out through my brothers' doors, the thought that one day I would have a record player or a guitar of my own seemed almost unbelievable. My brother Robert knew this and he knew what I was like. That was why when he went out, he always remembered to lock his bedroom door – he didn't want me going in there and messing with his stuff or playing his records and scratching them. Not only did he have a load of great records, but he also had an acoustic guitar. His room, to me, was a magical treasure trove.

All this was much too enticing and there was no way I was going to allow a locked door to keep me out. His room was on the first floor, but the roof on the lounge below used to jut out, so I could climb up onto the lounge roof and from there, I could reach his window and get in that way. When he locked the door and went out, I would climb into his room through the window and then play his records or play with his guitar until he got back. I didn't know how to play the guitar, of course, but that didn't matter – I used to imagine that I could play. I wasn't sent to piano lessons. I didn't study music formally. I just pretended until it was real.

The world of music, I understood, was older than the world of things. Music was older than our house and older than Liverpool. It was older than people and older than the dinosaurs. The birds sang in the air and the whales sang in the oceans long before our monkey ancestors became anything like humans. Long after we're gone, the music of the spheres will still ring out across the cosmos. Gods and religions are mayflies in comparison to music. Nations come and go. Empires are nothing. Only music remains: music and the silence that it emerges from.

I learnt all that as a kid, as I sat rapt in front of my brother's brown wooden speakers. It's what has guided me ever since. Through all of life's difficulties, in all the decisions that I have made, behind all that I've done and achieved, is the question, 'Is this what the music wants?' That's the North Star, the fixed point, around which all decisions make sense.

Music needs us to help it live up to its potential. We build it and it builds us. It needs us and we need it. I don't know why this is, I just know that's how it is. I know this because I sat in front of speakers as a little kid. I listened and that's what I heard. From that, all else followed.

'And there will always be anarchy in my heart,

I hope that the end for me can live up to the start.'

ACKNOWLEDGEMENTS

A special thank you to John Higgs for his talent and empathy in helping capture these moments.

Thanks to Riley Broudie, Pete Selby and Charlie Brotherstone for all the energy and time they've put in to making sure this book happened. And to everyone I've ever encountered personally or professionally ... sorry and thanks!